*Published by the National Institute of Adult Continuing Education
(England and Wales)
21 De Montfort Street
(Tel: 0116 2044200)*

© *NIACE 1999*

*British Library Cataloguing-in-Publication Data
A catalogue record for this book is available from the British Library
ISBN 1 86201 076 5
ISSN 0955-5374*

*All rights reserved. No part of this publication may be reproduced,
stored in a retrieval system or transmitted in any form or by any
means, electronic, mechanical, photocopying, recording or
otherwise, without prior permission in writing to NIACE.*

Every effort has been made to ensure the accuracy of the contents
of this publication. However, the information for this edition was
collected during October 1999 and there may well be alterations to
the dates, prices and locations of the learning holidays listed here.
The organisers and NIACE expressly disclaim responsibility in
law for negligence or any other cause of action.

*Compiled by Parin Moledina
Text set in 8 on 9pt Univers by The Midlands Book Typesetting
Company, Loughborough
Cover design by Richard Thumpston (Tel 0116 270 5371)
Printed and bound in Great Britain by Polestar Wheatons Ltd., Exeter
Distributed by Central Books Ltd., 99 Wallis Road, London E9 5LN*

Contents

- 4   Choosing your Learning Holiday
- 7   Learning Holiday Organisers
- 13   Index to Advertisers

Summer Learning Holidays in Britain

- 15   April 2000
- 32   May 2000
- 50   June 2000
- 73   July 2000
- 85   ARCA Supplement
- 100   August 2000
- 121   September 2000

Study Tours and Learning Holidays Abroad

- 139   April–September 2000
- 153   **Time to Learn** Order Form
- 155   Enquiry Forms
- 157   Subject Index

Published by the
National Institute of
Adult Continuing Education

How to choose your holiday using
TIME TO LEARN

This edition covers from April 2000 – September 2000 inclusive.

Learning holidays at centres in Britain are listed in date order starting on page 15.

Study tours and learning holidays abroad are listed separately in date order starting on page 139.

If you have a special interest in mind
Each learning holiday is allocated a number. If you wish to look for a specific course (e.g. Photography), look in the subject index starting on page 157 and it will give you a series of **course numbers** which you can then look up in the book.

What will it cost?
The fee quoted is only a guide to the price of tuition, accommodation and meals. You may find there are additional charges for such items as materials used, boat trips and entrance charges. An **AFD** in the fee column means **Ask For Details** and means that the organiser will supply you with details on request.

Conditions of booking
Always read these carefully before booking your learning holiday. Each centre has its own policy for **deposits, cancellations** and **refunds**. These are usually stated on the booking form.
It is advisable to arrange **insurance cover** against loss of fees due to cancellation.

Travel insurance is also required for study tours abroad and this is usually an additional charge. Please check that the policy provides adequate cover for all your needs.

For people with a physical disability ♿
Some centres have access for wheelchairs, ground floor bedrooms or lifts. Centres offering such facilities are marked with the **wheelchair symbol** in the address list for organisers.

For people with a visual impairment 👁
The **half-shaded eye symbol** is an indication of those centres who welcome people with a visual impairment to join their learning holidays.

For people with a hearing impairment 👂
A few centres can accommodate people with a hearing impairment. The **ear symbol** appears against those organisers.

We advise you to discuss all your needs with centres before booking.

A note from the publisher

NIACE makes every effort to compile the information in this directory accurately. We publish *Time to Learn* to promote the immense range and diversity of residential learning opportunities available in Britain and abroad.

However, NIACE is unable to investigate or accept any responsiblity for the content, organisation or conduct of the learning holidays listed here.

Please direct all comments and enquiries to the appropriate centres. Names, addresses and telephone numbers of all the contributing organisers are listed, beginning on page 7.

Please remember to mention that you found the information in TIME TO LEARN

Time to Learn

Summer Academy Study Holidays for the New Millennium

Choose from 108 study holidays. Themes include:

- **The Arts**
- **Countryside**
- **Heritage**
- **Personal Development**

Summer Academy
Keynes College (TL2000)
The University
Canterbury
Kent CT2 7NP

24 Hour Brochure Service
01227 470402
Fax: 01227 784338

Learning Holiday Organisers

♿ = Facilities for people with a physical disability
👁 = People with a visual impairment welcome
🎧 = People with a hearing impairment welcome
ARCA = Member of the *Adult Residential Colleges Association*

Abergavenny 'the Hill' Campus*
Pen-y-pound
Abergavenny
NP7 7RP
Tel: 01495 333777
Fax: 01495 333778
ARCA
(**previously known as The Hill*)

Acorn Activities
PO Box 120
Hereford
HR4 8YB
Tel: 01432 830083
Fax: 01432 830110
e-mail: info@acornactivities.co.uk
http://www.acornactivities.co.uk

Alston Hall Residential College ♿ 👁
Alston Lane
Longridge
Preston, Lancs, PR3 3BP
Tel: 01772 784661
Fax: 01772 785835
e-mail: enquiries@alstonhall.u-net.com
Website: http://www.alstonhall.u-net.com
ARCA

Ammerdown Centre ♿ 👁
Ammerdown
Radstock
Bath BA3 5SW
Tel: 01761 433709
Fax: 01761 433094
Loop system for hard of hearing

Belstead House
Education and Conference Centre
Belstead
Ipswich
Suffolk IP8 3NA
Tel: 01473 686321
Fax: 01473 686664
e-mail: belsteadhouse@talk21.com
ARCA

Benslow Music Trust
Little Benslow Hills
Benslow Lane
Hitchin
Herts SG4 9RB
Tel: 01462 459446
Fax: 01462 440171
e-mail: BmusicT@aol.com
ARCA

Birkbeck College
University of London
Faculty of Continuing Education
26 Russell Square
London WC1B 5DQ
Tel: 020 7631 6633 (6687 – 24 hours – Answerphone)
Fax: 020 7631 6688
e-mail: info@bbk.ac.uk
URL: http://www.bbk.ac.uk/

Brasshouse Centre
50 Sheepcote Street
Birmingham B16 8AJ
Tel: 0121 303 0114
Fax: 0121 303 4782
e-mail: brasshouse@easynet.co.uk
www.birmingham.gov.uk/brasshouse/

The British Institute of Florence
Piazza Strozzi 2
50123 Firenze
Italy
Tel: 0039 055 26778200
Fax: 0039 055 26778222

Burton Manor College
Burton
Neston
Cheshire CH64 5SJ
Tel: 0151 336 5172
Fax: 0151 336 6586
ARCA

The Charente Activity Centre
Le Poulailler
16210 St Romain
France
Tel/Fax: 00 33 5 45 98 63 92

Dillington House
Ilminster
Somerset
TA19 9DT
Booking Secretary: Tel: 01460 258613
Tel: 01460 52427
Fax: 01460 52433
ARCA

The Earnley Concourse
Earnley
Chichester
Sussex
PO20 7JL
Tel: 01243 670392
Fax: 01243 670832
e-mail: info@earnley.co.uk
www.earnley.co.uk

Edinburgh College of Art
Summer School, Continuing Studies
Lauriston Place
Edinburgh EH3 9DF
Tel: 0131 221 6111
Fax/24 hr tel: 0131 221 6109
e-mail: continuing.studies@eca.ac.uk
Internet: http://www.eca.ac.uk

Field Studies Council (FSC)
Head Office
Preston Montford
Shrewsbury
SY4 1HW
Tel: 01743 850674
Fax: 01743 850178
e-mail: fsc.headoffice@ukonline.co.uk
www.field-studies.council.org

FSC Overseas
Montford Bridge
Shrewsbury
SY4 1HW
Tel: 01743 850164 and 850522 (24 hrs)
Fax: 01743 850599
e-mail: fsc.overseas@ukonline.co.uk
http://www.fscOverseas.mcmail.com

The Greek Experience
19 Leopold Street
Southsea
Hampshire PO4 0JZ
Tel: 02392 830312
Fax: 02392 796047
e-mail: info@greekexperience.com
Website: http://www.greekexperience.com

Hawkwood College
Painswick Old Road
Stroud
Gloucestershire
GL6 7QW
Tel: 01453 759034
Fax: 01453 764607
e-mail: hawkwood@compuserve.com
ARCA

Hawthorn Bridge
8 Pond Close
Harefield
Middlesex
UB9 6NG
Tel: 01895 824240

HF Holidays Limited
Imperial House
Edgware Road
London
NW9 5AL
Tel: 0800 980 1324
Fax: 020-8205 0506
e-mail: info@hfholidays.co.uk

Higham Hall
Bassenthwaite Lake
Cockermouth
Cumbria
CA13 9SH
Tel: 017687 76276
Fax: 017687 76013
e-mail: higham.hall@dial.pipex.com
Internet: www.higham-hall.org.uk
Hearing loop available
ARCA

Horncastle College
Mareham Road
Horncastle
Lincs
LN9 6BW
Tel: 01507 522449
Fax: 01507 524382
e-mail: horncastle.college@lincolnshire.gov.uk
ARCA

Jackdaws Educational Trust
Bridge House
Great Elm
Frome
Somerset
BA11 3NY
Tel: 01373 812383
Fax: 01373 812083

Knuston Hall Residential College
Irchester
Wellingborough
Northants
NN29 7EU
Tel: 01933 312104
Fax: 01933 357596
e-mail: enquiries@knustonhall.org.uk
w.w.w.-http://www.knustonhall.org.uk
ARCA

L'Age Baston Holidays
Château L'Age Baston
St Projet St Constant
Charente
France
Tel: 0033 5 45 63 53 07
Fax: 0033 5456 30903
e-mail: LageBaston@aol.com

Lampeter Summer Workshop in Greek and Latin
Department of Classics
University of Wales, Lampeter
Lampeter
Ceredigion
SA48 7ED
Tel: 01570 424723
Fax: 01570 423877
e-mail: anne@lamp.ac.uk
http://www.lamp.ac.uk/classics

Lancashire College
Southport Road
Chorley
Lancashire
PR7 1NB
Tel: 01257 260909
Fax: 01257 241370
e-mail: insight@lancscollege.u-net.com
www.learningbreaks.org.uk
ARCA

Lancaster University
Department of Continuing Education
Lonsdale College
Lancaster
LA1 4YN
Tel: 01524 592624
Fax: 01524 592448
e-mail: conted@lancaster.ac.uk
http://www.lancs.ac.uk.users.conted/

Les Arts Vivants Sarl
Château Monferrier
24330 St Pierre de Chignac
Dordogne
France
Tel: 00 33 5 53 06 75 36
Fax: 00 33 5 53 06 08 82

Lindsey-Ward Print-making and Ceramics
Hey Cottage
64 Back Lane
Holmfirth
West Yorks
HD7 1HG
Tel: 01484 683428

Maryland College
Woburn
Bedfordshire
MK17 9JD
Tel: 01525 292901
Fax: 01525 290856
ARCA

Meirionnydd Languages
Bodyfuddau
Trawsfynydd
Gwynedd
LL41 4UW
Tel: 01766 540553
Website: meirionnydd.force9.co.uk

Missenden Abbey
Chilterns Continuing Education
Consortium Office
The Misbourne Centre
Great Missenden
Bucks
HP16 0BN
Tel: 01494 862904
Fax: 01494 890087
e-mail: enquiries@missendenabbey.ac.uk
Internet: www.aredu.org.uk/missendenabbey
ARCA

Oideas Gael
Gleann Cholm Cille
County Donegal
Southern Ireland
Tel: 00 353 73 30248
Fax: 00 353 73 30348
e-mail: oidsgael@iol.ie
www.Oideas-Gael.com

The Old Rectory
Fittleworth
Pulborough
Sussex
RH20 1HU
Tel/Fax: 01798 865306
ARCA

Pendrell Hall College of Residential Adult Education
Codsall Wood
Nr. Wolverhampton
WV8 1QP
Tel: 01902 434112
Fax: 01902 434113
e-mail: pendrell.college@staffordshire.gov.uk
Website: http://www.aredu.org.uk/pendrellhall
ARCA

Summer Academy
Keynes College
The University
Canterbury
Kent
CT2 7NP
Tel: 01227 470402/823473
Fax: 01227 784338

The University of Birmingham
School of Continuing Studies
Edgbaston
Birmingham
B15 2TT
Tel: 0121 414 5605/5607 (24 hours)
Fax: 0121 414 5619

University of Cambridge
Board of Continuing Education
Madingley Hall
Madingley
Cambridge
CB3 8AQ
Tel: 01954 280399
Fax: 01954 280200

University of Edinburgh
Centre for Continuing Education
11 Buccleuch Place
Edinburgh
Scotland
EH8 9LW
Tel: 0131 650 4400
Fax: 0131 667 6097
e-mail: CCE@ed.ac.uk
http://www.cce.ed.ac.uk

University of Liverpool
Centre for Continuing Education
19 Abercromby Square
Liverpool
L69 7ZG
Tel: 0151 794 2550/6900
Fax: 0151 794 2544

University of Manchester
Centre for Continuing Education
Oxford Road
Manchester
M13 9PL
Tel: 0161 275 3275
Fax: 0161 275 3300

University of Nottingham
School of Continuing Education
Special Programmes
Jubilee Campus
Nottingham
NG8 1BB
Tel: 0115 951 6526
Fax: 0115 951 6556

University of Wales, Swansea
Adult Continuing Education
Continuing Education Centre
Singleton Park
Swansea
SA2 8PP
Tel: 01792 295786
Fax: 01792 295751
e-mail: adult.education@swansea.ac.uk

Urchfont Manor College
Urchfont
Devizes
Wiltshire
SN10 4RG
Tel: 01380 840495
Fax: 01380 840005
ARCA

Wansfell College
Theydon Bois
Epping
Essex
CM16 7LF
Tel: 01992 813027
Fax: 01992 814761
e-mail: enrol@wansfell.demon.co.uk
Internet: http://www.aredu.demon.co.uk/wansfellcollege
ARCA

Wedgwood Memorial College
Station Wood
Barlaston
Stoke-on-Trent ST12 9DG
Tel: 01782 372105, 373427
Fax: 01782 372393
e-mail:
wedgwood.college@staffordshire.gov.uk
Website: http://www.aredu.org.uk/wedgwoodcollege
ARCA

Wensum Lodge
King Street
Norwich NR1 1QW
Tel: 01603 666021/2
Fax: 01603 765633
ARCA

Weobley Art Centre
(*Watercolour Weeks at Weobley*)
The Old Corner House
Weobley
Herefordshire
HR4 8SA
Tel/Fax: 01544 318548
Tel: 01544 319197
e-mail: enquiries@weobley.demon.co.uk
ARCA

West Dean College
West Dean
Chichester
West Sussex
PO18 0QZ
Tel: 01243 811301
Fax: 01243 811343
e-mail: westdean@pavilion.co.uk
ARCA

Residential Music Courses

Benslow is the unique centre for the study and practice of music. Our programme offers over 100 courses a year catering for both the experienced and less experienced musician. We provide expert tuition from visiting professional musicians, many of them distinguished figures from the major educational establishments and international music world. Choose from day, weekend, midweek and weeklong courses, including eight weeks of summer schools:

Choral and Solo Singing, Theory, Alexander Technique, Big Band, Recorder, Orchestras, Jazz, String Quartets, Saxophone, Harp, Baroque Opera, Solo and Ensemble Wind, Brass Ensembles, Keyboards and Piano

Send for a copy of our full programme brochure

BENSLOW MUSIC TRUST

Little Benslow Hills, Off Benslow Lane, Hitchin, Herts SG4 9RB

Tel: 01462 459446      Fax: 01462 440171
Email: BMusicT@aol.com

ARCA

Registered Charity No. 313663   Supported by the proceeds of the National Lottery through the Arts Council of England

Time to Learn

Index to Advertisers

Abergavenny 'the Hill' Campus	108	L'Age Baston Holidays	142
Acorn Activities	17, 93	Lancashire College	22
Alston Hall Residential College	126	Lancaster University	113
Ammerdown Centre	70	Les Arts Vivants	142
ARCA Colleges	85–88	Lindsey-Ward Print making and Ceramics	108
Belstead House	13	Maryland College	60
Benslow Music Trust	12	Meirionnydd Languages	122
Birbeck College	76	Missenden Abbey	44
Brass House Centre	70	Oideas Gael	148
British Institute of Florence	148	The Old Rectory	37
Burton Manor College	103	Pendrell Hall College of Residential Adult Education	108
Charente Activity Centre	148	Summer Academy	6
Dillington House	14	University of Birmingham	98
Earnley Concourse	48, 81	University of Cambridge	55
Edinburgh College of Art	98	University of Edinburgh	98
Field Studies Council	122	University of Nottingham	30
Greek Experience	142	Urchfont Manor College	30
Hawkwood College	117	Wansfell College	133
HF Holidays	70	Watercolour Weeks at Weobley	44
Higham Hall	65	Wedgwood Memorial College	60
Horncastle College	25	Wensum Lodge	117
Jackdaws	22	West Dean College	113
Knuston Hall Residential College	126		

Belstead House

Education & Conference Centre
Belstead,
Ipswich,
Suffolk IP8 3NA

LEARN AT LEISURE

- A warm welcome and a tranquil atmosphere
- Good food and good company
- Interesting courses all year round
- Easy access by road and rail

Tel: 01473 686321   Fax: 01473 686664
email: belsteadhouse@talk21.com

 Suffolk County Council *Education*

DILLINGTON HOUSE

DISCOVER THE SECRET OF BEAUTIFUL SOUTH SOMERSET

Discover and share in the secret of beautiful South Somerset and of Dillington House, Somerset's residential centre for adult education. A sixteenth century manor house and mews complex superbly refurbished with en-suite accommodation. Surrounded by mature parkland Dillington was once the home of George III's Prime Minister, Lord North. Now Dillington is the home of residential adult education in Somerset. It is the perfect learning environment – relaxing, beautiful, gracious, quiet, safe... and marvellously equipped for its modern purpose. The adult education programme offers a varied and heady mix of weekend courses, short-break courses, dayschools, public lectures and classical music concerts.

Treat yourself to the ultimate learning experience! Dillington House has nearly fifty years of experience in organising first class courses, engaging excellent tutors, providing superb food and generally ensuring that a stay at Dillington is memorable and rewarding... all this at prices which represent excellent value!

Why not visit our website to find out more, www.dillington.co.uk

Dillington House, just outside of Ilminster is easily accessed from the M5/J25 and the A303.

ARCA
Adult Residential Colleges Association

For a FREE programme about Dillington House and details of all our courses and events telephone (01460) 258613.

Summer Learning Holidays in Great Britain

■ ■ ■ ■

April 2000

☐ ☐ ☐ ☐

April
1 Pottery and print making: basics and beginnings in Summer Wineland £AFD

Lindsey-Ward Print-Making and Ceramics *Holmfirth, West Yorkshire*

1–2 April
2 Silversmithing £AFD
3 Pottery £AFD

Acorn Activities *Herefordshire*

1–3 April
4 Painting £84

HF Holidays *Haytor, Devon*

1–30 April
5 Russian – individual tuition* £AFD
6 French – individual tuition* £AFD
7 Beginners' Welsh – individual tuition* £AFD

Meirionnydd Languages *Trawsfynydd, Gwynedd*
£50 per day, subject to availability. Reduced fees for groups of 2/3 people

1–2 April
8 Aspects of Japanese art and culture £58/78

Maryland College *Woburn*
ARCA

2–5 April
9 An introduction to copper-plate calligraphy £AFD

West Dean College *Chichester*
ARCA

2–6 April
10 Map and compass £199

HF Holidays *Brecon*

2–6 April
11 Silk painting workshop £AFD

West Dean College *Chichester*
ARCA

2–7 April
12 Bridge £199

HF Holidays *Dovedale*

2–7 April
13 Next stage painting £AFD
14 Willow sculpture £AFD

Higham Hall *Cockermouth*
ARCA

2–7 April
15 Painting: new look – new ideas £AFD
16 Portrait heads in terracotta £AFD
17 Botanical illustration in spring £AFD

West Dean College *Chichester*
ARCA

3–6 April
18 Recorder rendezvous £125/150
Benslow Music Trust *Hitchin*
ARCA

3–7 April
19 Spring watercolours £298
20 Quilting £298
The Earnley Concourse *Chichester, Sussex*

3–7 April
21 Scottish country dancing – level 3 £174
HF Holidays *Malhamdale*

3–9 April
22 The beatitudes and colour £225
Ammerdown Centre *Radstock, Bath*

6–9 April
23 The Pre-Raphaelites in London £AFD
Univ Birmingham *London*

7–9 April
24 Bobbin and needle lace £90
25 Monks, sheep and drains £90
26 Chinese brush painting £90
Alston Hall College *Preston*
ARCA

7–9 April
27 The gods of ancient Egypt £78/98
Belstead House *Ipswich*
ARCA

7–9 April
28 Relax your voice £106/126
29 Bach for pianists £106/126
30 Millennium music £101/121
Benslow Music Trust *Hitchin*
ARCA

7–9 April
31 Britain's Changing Counryside £105
32 Bookbinding £105
Burton Manor College *Neston, Cheshire*
ARCA

7–9 April
33 Develop your silk painting skills £90/120
34 Bach 250: a celebratory study weekend £100/130
35 Meditation to quieten the mind £90/120
Dillington House *Ilminster*
ARCA

7–9 April
36 The musical world of Gainsborough's and Zoffany's pictures £158
37 Drawing and painting for beginners £158
38 Introduction to handwriting analysis £158
39 The countryside in spring £168
40 Cooking and eating the Japanese way £158
41 Using MS Word level 1 £188
42 Botanical illustration £158
The Earnley Concourse *Chichester, Sussex*

7–9 April
43 Improve your watercolours £89/114
Field Studies Council *Flatford Mill, Essex*

7–9 April
44 Lichens near London £89/114
Field Studies Council *Juniper Hall Centre, Dorking, Surrey*

7–9 April
45 Tassel and cord making £AFD
46 Virginia Woolf £AFD
47 Beethoven – the years of crisis £AFD
Higham Hall *Cockermouth*
ARCA

acorn*activities*

For Britain's **best** Learning Breaks

All-year activity & special interest holidays nationwide. Holidays for singles, couples, families and groups. Corporate Entertainment and Gift Vouchers available. Hotels, Guest Houses, Farmhouse accommodation available.

IT'S NEVER TOO LATE TO LEARN OR IMPROVE YOUR SKILL

OVER 50 ARTS & CRAFTS	**GARDEN DESIGN**
PAINTING & DRAWING	**WALKING & CYCLING**
COUNTRY SPORTS	**BALL SPORTS**
AIR SPORTS	**WATER SPORTS**
MOTOR SPORTS	**SPECIALIST PURSUITS**

FOR YOUR FREE BROCHURE WITH OVER 100 ACTIVITIES CALL NOW ON

01432 830083

acorn*activities*

PO BOX 120, HEREFORD HR4 8YB
TEL: 01432 830083 · FAX 01432 830110
www.acornactivities.co.uk
info@acornactivities.co.uk

7–9 April
48 Creative gardening £AFD
Horncastle College *Horncastle*
ARCA

7–9 April
49 A charm of cellists £105*
Jackdaws Educational Trust *Frome, Somerset*
*food included. B & B extra

7–9 April
50 World War I £107
51 Embroidery £107
52 Folk music weekend £107
53 Chinese brush painting £107
Knuston Hall *Irchester*
ARCA

7–9 April
54 Family learning break £AFD
Lancashire College *Chorley*
ARCA

7–9 April
55 Calligraphy – all levels £89/115
56 Diaghilev and the Ballet Russe £89/115
57 Retreat, relax, appraise £89/115
Maryland College *Woburn*
ARCA

7–9 April
58 Drawing workshop £AFD
59 Diaghilev and music £AFD
60 A weekend for recorder players £AFD
The Old Rectory *Fittleworth*
ARCA

7–9 April
61 Gold leaf calligraphy £AFD
Pendrell Hall College *Staffs*
ARCA

7–9 April
62 Reading Latin £80/129
63 Russian weekend £80/129
64 The three ages of opera II (1800–1900) £80/129
65 The Cretan labyrinth: the history of the Minoan civilisation £80/129
Univ Cambridge *Madingley, Cambridge*

7–9 April
66 The novels of D H Lawrence £AFD
67 Creative papier mache £AFD
68 Classic British film studios £AFD
Urchfont Manor College *Devizes*
ARCA

7–9 April
69 German language through literature – intermediate to advanced £96
70 Three poets of the Millennium: Dante, Chaucer, Pushkin £89
71 Learn to play the mandolin in a weekend £89
72 Music for mandolin ensemble £89
Wansfell College *Theydon Bois*
ARCA

7–9 April
73 Dynamic designers: pioneering women potters of the C20th £78
Wedgwood Memorial College Barlaston
ARCA

7–9 April
74 Understanding watercolour £215
Watercolour Weeks at Weobley
Weobley, Hereford

7–9 April
75 Cabinet making – part 1 £AFD
76 Further techniques in miniature painting £AFD
77 Further techniques in mosaic £AFD
78 Creative watercolour for beginners and improvers £AFD
79 Introduction to silversmithing £AFD
80 Honiton lace for all levels or needlelace for beginners £AFD
West Dean College *Chichester*
ARCA

April — Time to Learn — April

7–10 April
81 Exploring the seashore £117/150
Field Studies Council *Dale Fort Centre, Pembrokeshire*

7–10 April
82 Introduction to meditation £124
HF Holidays *Conistonwater*
83 Introduction to counselling £124
HF Holidays *Dovedale*
84 Isle of Wight on a bike £129
HF Holidays *Freshwater Bay*
85 Introduction to bridge £94
HF Holidays *Thurlestone Sands*

7–14 April
86 Art of living. Healing breath workshop £240
Ammerdown Centre *Radstock, Bath*

7–19 April
87 Dancing in the dark – workshop for couples £70/102
Hawkwood College *Stroud, Glos*
ARCA

8–9 April
88 Gourmet cookery £AFD
89 Decorative interiors and paint effects £AFD
Acorn Activities *Herefordshire*
90 Pottery £AFD
Acorn Activities *Scotland*

8–9 April
91 Japanese residential weekend £52/143
Brasshouse Language Courses *Birmingham*

8–11 April
92 Bridge – better card play £109
HF Holidays *Derwentwater*
93 Painting outdoors, indoors £129
HF Holidays *St Ives*

9–12 April
94 Map and compass £177
95 Painting outdoors, indoors £144
HF Holidays *Haytor, Devon*

9–13 April
96 Hieroglyphics £AFD
Higham Hall *Cockermouth*
ARCA

9–14 April
97 Painting landscapes and flowers £AFD
Higham Hall *Cockermouth*
ARCA

9–14 April
98 Silversmithing and jewellery £AFD
99 Drawing and painting landscape £AFD
100 Creative blacksmithing £AFD
101 Watercolour for improvers £AFD
102 Decorative tassels, ropes, cords and woven braids £AFD
West Dean College *Chichester*
ARCA

10–12 April
103 Retired citizens course £AFD
Pendrell Hall College *Staffs*
ARCA

10–12 April
104 Introduction to golf £89
Wansfell College *Theydon Bois*
ARCA

10–14 April
105 Better bridge: improve your scores £298
The Earnley Concourse *Chichester, Sussex*

10–14 April
106 Drawing cartoons £169
HF Holidays *Dovedale*

April — Time to Learn

10–14 April
107	Painting spring	£AFD
108	Rambles and relaxation	£AFD
109	Painting flowers and small creatures the Chinese way	£AFD

The Old Rectory *Fittleworth*
ARCA

10–15 April
110	Yoga	£219

HF Holidays *Derwentwater*

11–13 April
111	Introduction to calligraphy	£78

Wedgwood Memorial College
Barlaston
ARCA

11–14 April
112	Earth energy	£134

HF Holidays *St Ives*

11–15 April
113	Bridge – better bidding	£144

HF Holidays *Derwentwater*

12–14 April
114	Introduction to bridge	£88

HF Holidays *Alnmouth*

12–14 April
115	Sketching	£AFD

Pendrell Hall College *Staffs*
ARCA

14–16 April
116	Astronomy	£90
117	Elizabethan images (embroidery)	£90

Alston Hall College *Preston*
ARCA

14–16 April
118	Sherlock Holmes and the Victorian detective	£78/98
119	Ancient woodlands of Suffolk	£78/98
120	Seasons and weather in acrylics	£78/98

Belstead House *Ipswich*
ARCA

14–16 April
121	Russian music – yesterday and today	£110
122	China painting borders	£105
123	Colour, flowers and fragrance for health and well being	£125

Burton Manor College *Neston, Cheshire*
ARCA

14–16 April
124	Silk painting	£158
125	Progress with pastels	£158
126	Discover massage	£158
127	Poetry	£158
128	Bread and yeast cookery	£158
129	Our glorious garden heritage	£168
130	Introduction to the PC	£188

The Earnley Concourse *Chichester, Sussex*

14–16 April
131	First steps into landscape photography	£85/115
132	Stone circles	£85/115

Field Studies Council *Blencathra, Lake District*

14–16 April
133	Living off the land	£87/112
134	Introduction to bird watching in the southern Lakes	£87/112

Field Studies Council *Castle Head Centre, Lake District*

April — Time to Learn — April

14–16 April
135 Otters and other
    riverside mammals   £89/114
136 Family birdwatching at
    Minsmere and Flatford   £AFD
137 Drawing and painting for
    families   £AFD
**Field Studies Council *Flatford Mill,
Essex***

14–16 April
138 Hedgerow baskets   £90/120
**Field Studies Council *Preston
Montford, Shropshire***

14–16 April
139 Creative paper making £97/131
**Hawkwood College *Stroud, Glos*
ARCA**

14–16 April
140 The Celts in Cumbria   £AFD
**Higham Hall *Cockermouth*
ARCA**

14–16 April
141 Lincolnshire wold   £AFD
**Horncastle College *Horncastle*
ARCA**

14–16 April
142 Harp weekend   £105*
**Jackdaws Educational Trust *Frome,
Somerset***
*food included. B & B extra

14–16 April
143 Bedfordshire lace –
    all levels   £107
144 From total collapse to
    economic miracle   £107
145 Calligraphy   £107
**Knuston Hall *Irchester*
ARCA**

14–16 April
146 Windows Housekeeping £AFD
147 Russian   £AFD
**Lancashire College *Chorle*
ARCA**

14–16 April
148 England at the end of
    the first millennium   £89/115
149 Two French novels:
    Balzac: *L'Illusion Perdue*
    and Butor: *La
    Modification*   £89/115
**Maryland College *Woburn*
ARCA**

14–16 April
150 Singing for the tone deaf £AFD
151 Calligraphy for absolute
    beginners   £AFD
152 Watercolour: the beguiling
    medium   £AFD
153 Early spring birds   £AFD
**The Old Rectory *Fittleworth*
ARCA**

14–16 April
154 Symbolism and epic
    drama   £80/129
155 Romanticism into
    Impressionism   £80/129
156 The black death   £80/129
157 Doing film history   £80/129
Univ Cambridge *Madingley, Cambridge*

14–16 April
158 How to be a travel writer £AFD
159 Classic guitar weekend   £AFD
160 Bedfordshire lace   £AFD
**Urchfont Manor College *Devizes*
ARCA**

14–16 April
161 Chinese bamboo pens
    and colour washes   £78
**Wedgwood Memorial College
Barlaston
ARCA**

Lancashire College

Lancashire College is a purpose built residential college with an international reputation for running adult courses. The College offers a wide choice of residential courses throughout the year, excellent facilities and expert tuition. Easily accessible by motorway, rail and air, Lancashire College is located close to the market town of Chorley. Courses are complemented by good food and a sociable and relaxed learning environment.

New for 2000

- Family Learning Breaks
- Personal Finance Toolkit
- Life Support courses

www.learningbreaks.org.uk

Free colour brochure from: Lancashire College, Southport Road, Chorley, PR7 1NB. Telephone 01257 260909
Fax 01257 241370 e-mail: insight@lancscollege.u-net.com

Jackdaws 2000
Residential Music Courses

Jackdaws' aim is to provide an inspirational setting for music lovers to discover for themselves that the deepest pleasure in music comes from understanding and hard work: Summer courses are held every weekend from April 28th – Sept 22nd

Tutors include:
Caecilia Andriessen	Paul Hamburger
Rae Woodland	Sarah Francis
Laura Sarti	Joy Mammen
Neil and Penny Jenkins	Philip Fowke
David Smith & Brenda Blewitt	Elizabeth Turnbull
George Hadjinikos	Penelope Cave
Noelle Barker	Elizabeth Andrews
	Victor Morris

***Brochures from* Jackdaws,** Bridge House, Great Elm, Frome, Somerset BA11 3NY
Tel: 01373 812383 Fax: 01373 812083 *Musical Director: Maureen Lehane Wishart*

14–16 April
162 Stickmaking (walking sticks, crooks and thumb sticks) £70/105
163 Super singing for non singers £70/105
Wensum Lodge *Norwich*
ARCA

14–16 April
164 Developing drawing and painting skills £AFD
165 Mozart and his operas (lectures) £AFD
166 Making dishes and wall-pieces £AFD
167 Dreams and fairy tales – a painting course £AFD
168 Elizabethan blackwork £AFD
169 Experimental batik on paper £AFD
West Dean College *Chichester*
ARCA

14–17 April
170 The fool and I: drama workshop £AFD
Hawkwood College *Stroud, Glos*
ARCA

14–17 April
171 Isle of Wight on a bike £129
HF Holidays *Freshwater Bay*
172 Classical music £134
HF Holidays *Malhamdale*
173 Alexander Technique £139
HF Holidays *Pitlochry*
174 The Tate in St Ives £114
175 Japanese garden design £159
HF Holidays *St Ives*
176 Total confidence £124
HF Holidays *Thurlestone Sands*

14–17 April
177 Landscape photography £AFD
West Dean College *Chichester*
ARCA

14–21 April
178 Countryside creatures £180/285
179 Drawing and painting in all media £180/285
Field Studies Council *Preston Montford, Shropshire*

14–21 April
180 Botanical illustration £AFD
Higham Hall *Cockermouth*
ARCA

15–16 April
181 Interior design £AFD
182 Drawing for the terrified £AFD
183 Gourmet cookery £AFD
Acorn Activities *Herefordshire*
184 Stained glass £AFD
185 Interior design £AFD
186 Gourmet cookery £AFD
Acorn Activities *Scotland*
187 Stained glass £AFD
Acorn Activities *Shropshire*
188 Garden design £AFD
Acorn Activities *Worcestershire*

15–16 April
189 The Peak District £AFD
Univ Manchester *Manchester*

15–18 April
190 Bridge – improvers £112
HF Holidays *Selworthy*

15–21 April
191 Bridge – improvers £214
HF Holidays *Selworthy*

16–18 April
192 Aurora Wind Ensemble £AFD
Hawkwood College *Stroud, Glos*
ARCA

16–19 April
193 Free machine embroidery £AFD
West Dean College *Chichester*
ARCA

16–21 April
194 Discovery and
 creation £130/180
Field Studies Council *Castle Head Centre, Lake District*

16–21 April
195 Wild flower week:
 the top 20 flower
 families £184/235
Field Studies Council *Flatford Mill, Essex*

16–21 April
196 Map and compass £257
197 Painting indoors £189
HF Holidays *Alnmouth*
198 Bridge – making
 conventions clear £184
199 Birthplace of the canals £234
HF Holidays *Dovedale*
200 Line dancing – level 3 £209
HF Holidays *Haytor, Devon*
201 Internet for beginners £319
HF Holidays *Whitby*

16–21 April
202 Small silverwork £AFD
Higham Hall *Cockermouth*
ARCA

16–21 April
203 Calligraphy £AFD
Knuston Hall *Irchester*
ARCA

16–21 April
204 Landscape painting in
 watercolour £AFD
205 Colour – in landscape
 and still life £AFD
West Dean College *Chichester*
ARCA

16–22 April
206 Painting pots and flowers £439
Watercolour Weeks at Weobley
Weobley, Hereford

17–19 April
207 Computers for beginners £188
Burton Manor College *Neston, Cheshire*
ARCA

17–19 April
208 Arts and crafts taster £AFD
209 Computing for absolute
 beginners £AFD
Lancashire College *Chorley*
ARCA

17–19 April
210 Digital photography £AFD
Urchfont Manor College *Devizes*
ARCA

17–20 April
211 Chamber music £140
Alston Hall College *Preston*
ARCA

17–20 April
212 Stained glass workshop £163
213 Flower painting in
 watercolour £152
Burton Manor College *Neston, Cheshire*
ARCA

17–20 April
214 Honiton lace £AFD
215 Lacemaking: English
 and Belgian £AFD
Urchfont Manor College *Devizes*
ARCA

17–21 April
216 The countryside in spring:
 a family wildlife discovery
 week £AFD
Field Studies Council *Juniper Hall Centre, Dorking, Surrey*

WIDE-RANGING ACTIVITY SHORT BREAKS IN THE HISTORIC MARKET TOWN OF HORNCASTLE

nestling on the edge of the Lincolnshire Wolds.

All inclusive rates for three days/two nights (including tuition, bed and breakfast, lunch, evening meal and light refreshments) from just £90.

All Year Round Short Breaks

LEARN for PLEASURE

Arts and Crafts	Healthy Living
Astronomy	Interior Design
Computing	Music
Conservation	
Countryside Interpretation	Rambling Breaks
Creative Writing	Travel Writers
Historic Field Trips	Watercolours

Phone now for a brochure on
01507 522449
Horncastle College, Mareham Road,
Horncastle, LN9 6BW.
Fax: 01507 524382
e-mail: horncastle.college@lincolnshire.gov.uk

LINCOLNSHIRE COUNTY COUNCIL

April — Time to Learn — April

17–21 April
217 Learn to play electronic keyboards £199
218 Painting – soft pastels indoors £194
HF Holidays Brecon
219 Ballroom dancing – level 1 £154
HF Holidays Conwy
220 Sequence dancing – level £144
HF Holidays Freshwater Bay
221 Island tour on a bike £144
HF Holidays Isle of Arran
222 C20th music £199
HF Holidays Malhamdale
223 Singing for pleasure £174
HF Holidays Pitlochry
224 Painting – still life £169
225 Four Nordic composers £169
HF Holidays St Ives
226 Introduction to Feng Shui £164
HF Holidays Thurlestone Sands

18–21 April
227 Bridge – improvers £109
HF Holidays Selworthy

19–26 April
228 Drawing and painting at Easter £201/262
229 Easter birds £225/286
Field Studies Council Nettlecombe Court Centre, Exmoor

19–28 April
230 Making musical instruments £AFD
West Dean College Chichester
ARCA

20–24 April
231 2000 years of shaping Britain (Easter) £199
Alston Hall College Preston
ARCA

20–24 April
232 Celebration of Holy Week and the Easter liturgy £160
Ammerdown Centre Radstock, Bath

20–24 April
233 Easter bridge £198
234 Easter painting workshop £198
235 Easter writing £198
Burton Manor College Neston, Cheshire
ARCA

20–24 April
236 Nature photography £152/194
Field Studies Council Orielton Centre, Pembrokeshire

20–24 April
237 Easter getaway weekend: crafts, arts, painting and other activities £AFD
The Old Rectory Fittleworth
ARCA

20–25 April
238 Renaissance music at Easter £250
Wedgwood Memorial College Barlaston
ARCA

21–23 April
239 Calligraphy, italic – formal and experimental £AFD
240 The spring garden in watercolour £AFD
West Dean College Chichester
ARCA

21–24 April
241 Spring birdwatching for the family £AFD
Field Studies Council Dale Fort Centre, Pembrokeshire

21–24 April
242 Family naturalist and bird course £AFD
Field Studies Council Preston Montford, Shropshire

21–24 April
243 The Higham weekend: an informal gathering for members of Friends of Higham £AFD
Higham Hall *Cockermouth*
ARCA

21–24 April
244 Ecclesiastic art and architecture to c1650 £120/193
Univ Cambridge *Madingley, Cambridge*

21–24 April
245 Full creative control of your SLR camera £AFD
West Dean College *Chichester*
ARCA

21–25 April
246 Birdwatching for families £AFD
Field Studies Council *Flatford Mill, Essex*

21–25 April
247 Birds of the borderland £129/172
Field Studies Council *Preston Montford, Shropshire*

21–25 April
248 Bridge – improvers £194
HF Holidays *Alnmouth*
249 Wildlife woodcarving £269
HF Holidays *Whitby*

21–26 April
250 Bookbinding for beginners and improvers £184/235
251 Improve your watercolours £184/235
Field Studies Council *Flatford Mill, Essex*

21–28 April
252 Trees and woodlands in the British countryside £273/350
Field Studies Council *Flatford Mill, Essex*

21–28 April
253 Landscape painting £180/285
Field Studies Council *Preston Montford, Shropshire*

21–28 April
254 Alberni masterclass £295/413
Univ Cambridge *Madingley, Cambridge*

22–24 April
255 Life drawing £100
Alston Hall College *Preston*
ARCA

23–26 April
256 Spring flower painting £AFD
West Dean College *Chichester*
ARCA

23–28 April
257 Pottery general – handbuilding and throwing £AFD
West Dean College *Chichester*
ARCA

23–29 April
258 Watercolour week £439
Watercolour Weeks at Weobley *Weobley, Hereford*

24–28 April
259 Fashion felts £185
260 Red rose rambles for springtime £199
261 Machine knitting £185
Alston Hall College *Preston*
ARCA

24–28 April

262 An introduction to birds and birdwatching £190
Ammerdown Centre *Radstock, Bath*

24–28 April

263 Exploring watercolours £298
264 Flower painting in watercolours £298
The Earnley Concourse *Chichester, Sussex*

24–28 April

265 Normans in the north £AFD
266 China restoration – beginners £AFD
267 Walk safely in the hills £AFD
Higham Hall *Cockermouth*
ARCA

24–28 April

268 Drawing workshop: variations on a subject £160/270
Univ Cambridge *Madingley, Cambridge*

24–28 April

269 Improving your colour photography £AFD
West Dean College *Chichester*
ARCA

24–30 April

270 Benslow baroque opera project £290/330
Benslow Music Trust *Hitchin*
ARCA

25–27 April

271 Introduction to aromatherapy £105
272 Demystify the Web £115
Burton Manor College *Neston, Cheshire*
ARCA

25–27 April

273 Golf: from beginner to competitor £89
274 Making weaves £89
275 Henry Moore – sculptor £99
Wansfell College *Theydon Bois*
ARCA

25–28 April

276 Flower painting £78/98
Belstead House *Ipswich*
ARCA

25–28 April

277 Tutankhamun rediscovered £135/180
278 The Monmouth rebellion £163/208
279 Painting on China £140/185
Dillington House *Ilminster*
ARCA

25–28 April

280 Canal boat art £AFD
Knuston Hall *Irchester*
ARCA

25–28 April

281 Creative weaving £AFD
282 Colour matching using acid dyes £AFD
283 Water colour painting £AFD
Urchfont Manor College *Devizes*
ARCA

25–28 April

284 Early music for recorder £121
285 Pastel drawing and painting £121
Wedgwood Memorial College *Barlaston*
ARCA

25–29 April

286 Bridge – improvers £186
HF Holidays *Alnmouth*

26–28 April
287 Spring birdwatch £105
Burton Manor College *Neston, Cheshire*
ARCA

27 April–1 May
288 The white cockade: Jacobite rebellions in Scotland £230
Univ Liverpool *Perth and Inverness*

28–30 April
289 Bedfordshire lace £90
290 Chamber choir £90
Alston Hall College *Preston*
ARCA

28–30 April
291 Local history weekend £78/98
Belstead House *Ipswich*
ARCA

28–30 April
292 Music made visible £105
Burton Manor College *Neston, Cheshire*
ARCA

28–30 April
293 Verdi – opera for all £90/120
294 An introduction to Alfred Hitchcock £90/120
295 Graphology – the hidden secrets of handwriting £90/120
Dillington House *Ilminster*
ARCA

28–30 April
296 Introduction to the Internet £188
The Earnley Concourse *Chichester, Sussex*

28–30 April
297 Camera skills: making your camera work for you £92/117
298 National Vegetation Classification: woodland habits £97/124
Field Studies Council *Flatford Mill, Essex*

28–30 April
299 Writing for pleasure £89/114
300 Exploring the river mole: a family discovery weekend £AFD
301 Grass identification in spring £97/124
Field Studies Council *Juniper Hall Centre, Dorking, Surrey*

28–30 April
302 Making your mark – artistic expression £AFD
303 Dru yoga £102/136
Hawkwood College *Stroud, Glos*
ARCA

28–30 April
304 Canal boat art £107
305 Creative writing £107
306 Reiki healing – first degree £107
307 Lacemaking £107
Knuston Hall *Irchester*
ARCA

28–30 April
308 Pamper weekend: a health and fitness taster £AFD
309 Canvas work for beginners and improvers £AFD
310 The Stock Market explained £AFD
Lancashire College *Chorley*
ARCA

URCHFONT MANOR
Residential College for Adult Education
Conference and Training Centre

▲ Urchfont Manor is a fine country house of mellow brick dating from the late seventeenth century, surrounded by ten acres of beautiful parkland. Readily accessible from the M4 to the north and the A303 to the south, it lies just outside the market town of Devizes in an area rich in prehistoric sites, grand stately homes and attractive villages.

▲ Urchfont offers a wide range of weekend, 4-day and 6-day courses throughout the year, covering history, archaeology, philosophy, writing, music appreciation, painting and drawing, and many crafts.

Details from: Urchfont Manor College,
Nr Devizes, Wiltshire SN10 4RG.
Tel: 01380–840495, Fax: 01380–840005.

UNIVERSITY OF NOTTINGHAM
LEARN AT LEISURE

Weekend Breaks
Campus Summer School
Study Tours Abroad

Enthusiastic Tutors
Exciting Venues
Enormous Subject Range

FREE brochure from:
Continuing Education, Special Programmes
Jubilee Campus, Nottingham, NG8 1BB
Tel: 0115 951 6526 Fax: 0115 951 6556

Time to Learn

April

28–30 April
311 Ancient cities of the Middle East £89/115
312 Introduction to computers £99/125
313 Sherlock Holmes and Victorian detection £89/115
Maryland College *Woburn*
ARCA

28–30 April
314 Reading classical Greek: advanced £80/129
315 Further geology £80/129
316 A history of China through its famous women £80/129
317 Life in Iron Age Britain £80/129
Univ Cambridge *Madingley, Cambridge*

28–30 April
318 The music of Rachmaninov £AFD
319 A voyage into writing £AFD
Urchfont Manor College *Devizes*
ARCA

28–30 April
320 The human voice on record £89
321 The navvy and his legacy £98
322 Introduction to computing £93
Wansfell College *Theydon Bois*
ARCA

28–30 April
323 Deutsch aktiv £77
324 Modern management and democracy at work £75
Wedgwood Memorial College
Barlaston
ARCA

28–30 April
325 Jewellery £AFD
326 Oil painting for beginners £AFD
327 An introduction to mosaic £AFD
West Dean College *Chichester*
ARCA

28 April–1 May
328 Painting and sketching £232
329 Spring into summer: health and fitness weekend £232
330 Stained glass £232
331 Get the best from your compact camera £232
332 Chinese wok cookery £232
333 Silk painting £232
The Earnley Concourse *Chichester, Sussex*

28 April–1 May
334 Stoneflies, mayflies and caddis: an identification workshop £113/165
Field Studies Council *Slapton Ley Centre, Devon*

28 April–1 May
335 The RSC £244
HF Holidays *Bourton-on-the-Water*
336 Painting – still life £154
HF Holidays *Dovedale*

28 April–1 May
337 The Tennyson Society weekend £AFD
Higham Hall *Cockermouth*
ARCA

28 April–1 May
338 Pianos for all £105*
Jackdaws Educational Trust *Frome, Somerset*
food included. B & B extra

28 April–1 May
339 The geology of the Lleyn peninsula £AFD
Univ Liverpool *Abersoch*

28 April–1 May
340 Relief stone carving £AFD
341 Cane, willow and rush seating, basketry £AFD
West Dean College *Chichester*
ARCA

| April | *Time to Learn* | May |

28 April–2 May
342 South Devon birds: sights and sounds of spring £125/160
Field Studies Council *Slapton Ley Centre, Devon*

29–30 April
343 Garden design £AFD
344 Dry stane dyking £AFD
Acorn Activities *Scotland*

29 April–3 May
345 Bridge – next step £206
HF Holidays *Brecon*
346 Painting seascapes £234
HF Holidays *St Ives*

29 April–6 May
347 Alexander Technique and walking £369
HF Holidays *Freshwater Bay*

30 April–3 May
348 Pastels in spring £135
Alston Hall College *Preston ARCA*

30 April–3 May
349 Yoga £149
HF Holidays *Selworthy*

30 April–5 May
350 Moving on with watercolour £AFD
West Dean College *Chichester ARCA*

30 April–6 May
351 Bridge – improvers £269
352 Line dancing – level 3 £274
HF Holidays *Conwy*

■ ■ ■ ■

May 2000

☐ ☐ ☐ ☐

May
353 Pottery and print making: basics and beginnings in Summer Wineland £AFD
Lindsey-Ward Print-Making and Ceramics *Holmfirth, West Yorkshire*

1–3 May
354 The kitchen garden for beginners £AFD
West Dean College *Chichester ARCA*

1–5 May
355 Painting £AFD
Higham Hall *Cockermouth ARCA*

1–5 May
356 Bookbinding and book restoration £AFD
Urchfont Manor College *Devizes ARCA*

1–6 May
357 English medieval architecture £314
HF Holidays *Bourton-on-the-Water*
358 Photography tour £289
HF Holidays *Dovedale*
359 Ballroom dancing – level 2 £264
HF Holidays *Haytor, Devon*

Time to Learn — May

1–31 May
360 Russian – individual tuition* £AFD
361 French – individual tuition* £AFD
362 Beginners' Welsh – individual tuition* £AFD
Meirionnydd Languages *Trawsfynydd, Gwynedd*
*£50 per day, subject to availability. Reduced fees for groups of 2/3 people

2–4 May
363 Watercolour painting – flowers £AFD
364 Writing autobiography £AFD
Lancashire College *Chorley*
ARCA

2–4 May
365 Chinese brush painting £96
Wansfell College *Theydon Bois*
ARCA

2–5 May
366 English country houses and their estates £160
Wedgwood Memorial College *Barlaston*
ARCA

3–5 May
367 Countryside in spring £100
Alston Hall College *Preston*
ARCA

3–5 May
368 Some aspects of German history and literature as seen on the cinema screen £89
Wansfell College *Theydon Bois*
ARCA

3–6 May
369 Nature and plant photography £194
370 Sussex on a bike £164
HF Holidays *Abingworth*

371 Scottish country dancing – level 1 £154
HF Holidays *Brecon*
372 Yoga £149
HF Holidays *Selworthy*

3–7 May
373 Helston Furry Dance £249
HF Holidays *St Ives*

5–6 May
374 Painting spring flowers £AFD
Urchfont Manor College *Devizes*
ARCA

5–7 May
375 Viol consort playing £90
376 Complementary therapies £95
Alston Hall College *Preston*
ARCA

5–7 May
377 String chamber music £126/146
Benslow Music Trust *Hitchin*
ARCA

5–7 May
378 Playing the recorder £90/120
Dillington House *Ilminster*
ARCA

5–7 May
379 Flower painting £158
380 Colourful calligraphy £158
381 How to write a successful novel £158
382 Introduction to astrology £158
383 Speak German – intermediate £158
384 Speak Italian – advanced £158
385 Using your PC £188
The Earnley Concourse *Chichester, Sussex*

5–7 May
386 Wild flowers of woodlands and hedgerows £89/114
387 Watercolour for absolute beginners £89/114
388 The National Trust in Suffolk: Lavenham, Melford and Orford Ness £89/114

May — Time to Learn

389 Drawing and sketching
for watercolour £89/114
390 Bird songs and calls £89/114
Field Studies Council *Flatford Mill, Essex*

5–7 May
391 Wild flowers for
beginners £97/124
Field Studies Council *Juniper Hall Centre, Dorking, Surrey*

5–7 May
392 Look out for mammals:
an identification
workshop £69/112
Field Studies Council *Rhyd-y-creuau Centre, Snowdonia*

5–7 May
393 Astrosophy – man and
the stars £60/92
**Hawkwood College *Stroud, Glos*
ARCA**

5–7 May
394 Singing for the tone deaf £AFD
395 Painting on silk and
velvet – beginners £AFD
**Higham Hall *Cockermouth*
ARCA**

5–7 May
396 Goldwork embroidery £AFD
397 Tai Chi £AFD
**Horncastle College *Horncastle*
ARCA**

5–7 May
398 Tracing those family
skeletons – research your
family tree £107
399 Psychology of man's
best friend £107
400 Flower painting £107
**Knuston Hall *Irchester*
ARCA**

5–7 May
401 Posters, pics, adverts –
graphic illustrations £AFD
402 French for absolute
beginners £AFD
403 Italian for absolute
beginners £AFD
404 Russian for absolute
beginners £AFD
405 Greek for absolute
beginners £AFD
406 Spanish for absolute
beginners £AFD
**Lancashire College *Chorley*
ARCA**

5–7 May
407 Nelson: the man and
his navy £72/166
408 C20th music £72/166
409 Writing nature poetry £72/166
410 Watercolour: C&G 7802 £72/166
411 Theatrical masks:
stitched or stuck £72/166
412 Goldwork embroidery £72/166
413 Pottery and porcelain
restoration: C&G 7802 £72/166
414 Embroidery: C&G
7900 – part one £72/166
415 Woodcarving: C&G
7802 and 7900 £72/166
416 The art of mosaic £72/166
**Missenden Abbey *Great Missenden*
ARCA**

5–7 May
417 The world of Spanish £AFD
418 Pastels in spring £AFD
419 Walking the Downs
and Weald £AFD
420 Alexander Technique £AFD
**The Old Rectory *Fittleworth*
ARCA**

5–7 May
421 Life painting £AFD
**Pendrell Hall College *Staffs*
ARCA**

5–7 May
422	More sources for genealogy	£80/129
423	Britten and Shostakovitch	£80/129
424	The world of the New Testament	£80/129
425	Insects and mini beasts	£80/129

Univ Cambridge *Madingley, Cambridge*

5–7 May
426	Spanish – advanced	£90
427	In the shadow of the Dome	£100
428	Relax with raffia	£94

Wansfell College *Theydon Bois*
ARCA

5–7 May
429	Great solo piano works of 19th/20th centuries	£80

Wedgwood Memorial College Barlaston
ARCA

5–7 May
430	Glass – textures for drill engravers	£AFD
431	Pottery – throwing and turning	£AFD
432	Life drawing	£AFD
433	Woodturning for beginners	£AFD

West Dean College *Chichester*
ARCA

5–8 May
434	Painting miniatures and silhouettes	£114/146

Field Studies Council *Juniper Hall Centre, Dorking, Surrey*

6–7 May
435	Silversmithing	£AFD
436	Pottery	£AFD

Acorn Activities *Herefordshire*
437	Mosaic	£AFD

Acorn Activities *Scotland*

6–9 May
438	T'ai chi	£204

HF Holidays *Isle of Arran*

6–10 May
439	Map and compass	£221

HF Holidays *Derwentwater*
440	Bowls	£194

HF Holidays *Selworthy*

6–13 May
441	Birdwatching	£389

HF Holidays *Conwy*
442	Walking with Ceilidh dancing	£329

HF Holidays *Freshwater Bay*
443	T'ai chi	£329

HF Holidays *Isle of Arran*

7–11 May
444	Landscape painting	£AFD

Urchfont Manor College *Devizes*
ARCA

7–12 May
445	Colour cloth	£AFD

Higham Hall *Cockermouth*
ARCA

7–12 May
446	From the cradle to the grave: for the visually impaired	£156

Wedgwood Memorial College Barlaston
ARCA

7–12 May
447	Painting – observation and imagination	£AFD
448	Cane, rush and willow work	£AFD

West Dean College *Chichester*
ARCA

7–13 May
449	Landscape painting	£364

HF Holidays *St Ives*

8–10 May
450	Copper and pewterwork	£89
451	The village syndrome and town and country planning in Britain	£99

Wansfell College *Theydon Bois* **ARCA**

8–10 May
452	Scented plants and scented gardens	£AFD

West Dean College *Chichester* **ARCA**

8–12 May
453	Batik: further skills	£298
454	Repairing and restoring china	£298
455	Walking Chichester harbour	£313

The Earnley Concourse *Chichester, Sussex*

8–12 May
456	Sculpture – carving and modelling in various media	£AFD
457	Spring flowers in watercolour and gouache	£AFD
458	Walking and bridge	£AFD

The Old Rectory *Fittleworth* **ARCA**

8–15 May
459	Landscape painting	£379

HF Holidays *Conistonwater*

9–11 May
460	Recorder playing	£AFD

Pendrell Hall College *Staffs* **ARCA**

10–12 May
461	Painting on china workshop	£103

Wansfell College *Theydon Bois* **ARCA**

10–13 May
462	Photography tour	£184

HF Holidays *Alnmouth*

463	Map and compass	£166

HF Holidays *Derwentwater*

464	T'ai chi	£154

HF Holidays *Isle of Arran*

465	Painting flowers indoors	£179

HF Holidays *Malhamdale*

466	Calligraphy	£144

HF Holidays *Thurlestone Sands*

10–17 May
467	Simply wild flowers	£218/280

Field Studies Council *Orielton Centre, Pembrokeshire*

11–14 May
468	The Roman West Country	£240

Univ Birmingham *Cirencester*

11–16 May
469	A disputed land: historic landscapes of the Hexham area	£AFD

Univ Liverpool *Yorkshire*

12–14 May
470	Wildlife weekend	£AFD

Acorn Activities *Pembrokeshire*

12–14 May
471	Silversmithing and goldsmithing	£135
472	Birdwatching	£100

Alston Hall College *Preston* **ARCA**

12–14 May
473	Foundation strings	£101/121
474	Solo singing weekend	£106/126

Benslow Music Trust *Hitchin* **ARCA**

THE OLD RECTORY, FITTLEWORTH
WEST SUSSEX

The Old Rectory is an attractive, family-run college set in beautiful countryside near the South Downs. Privately owned, the Old Rectory offers a particularly friendly and welcoming atmosphere in which to pursue a course of your choice.

The House dates in part from the 16th century, and has since been enlarged, and now offers extensive accommodation in single or twin rooms, many with private bathrooms. There is a licensed bar and two acres of delightful garden with swimming pool, and the surrounding countryside is ideal for walking.

A wide range of weekend, mid-week and week-long residential courses is held throughout the year. Subjects covered include: Painting (Watercolour, Oils, Pastels, Pen and Wash, Portraits, Landscape, Botanical illustration etc.), Crafts Chinese Brush Painting, Embroidery, Picture Framing, Stained Glass, Upholstery etc. Music Singing, Literature, Natural History, Computing and Word Processing, Walking, and many others.

The Old Rectory is also available as a conference centre for groups of up to 50. Details available on request.

For full course details please write or ring for our current brochure:

Tony & Sue Dawkins
The Old Rectory Adult Education College
Fittleworth, Pulborough, W. Sussex RH20 1HU.
Tel/Fax: 01798 865306

ARCA

12–14 May

475	Astronomy	£110
476	Reiki 1	£160

Burton Manor College *Neston, Cheshire*
ARCA

12–14 May

477	Painting on glass	£158
478	Drawing	£158
479	Discover yoga	£158
480	Better swimming	£158
481	Bridge for improvers: level 2	£158
482	Making and using handmade paper	£158
483	Introduction to the PC	£188

The Earnley Concourse *Chichester, Sussex*

12–14 May

484	Introduction to basket weaving	£100/130
485	Photographing people	£85/115

Field Studies Council *Blencathra, Lake District*

12–14 May

486	Family birdwatching at Minsmere and Flatford	£AFD
487	Spring walking weekend: exploring Constable Country	£89/114
488	Watercolour for near beginners	£89/114
489	Improve your oil painting	£89/114
490	Bird songs and calls	£89/114

Field Studies Council *Flatford Mill, Essex*

12–14 May

491	Birds and bird song in spring	£97/124
492	Tatting weekend	£89/114
493	Pooh sticks and rabbit holes: a family discovery weekend	£AFD

Field Studies Council *Juniper Hall Centre, Dorking, Surrey*

12–14 May

494	Great piano works of the 19th and 20th centuries	£AFD
495	Further studies in genealogy	£AFD

Higham Hall *Cockermouth*
ARCA

12–14 May

496	Piano workshop	£105*

Jackdaws Educational Trust *Frome, Somerset*
*food included. B & B extra

12–14 May

497	History alive – the Romans in Britain	£AFD

Lancashire College *Chorley*
ARCA

12–14 May

498	Belgian lacemaking	£89/115
499	Traditional jazz	£89/115

Maryland College *Woburn*
ARCA

12–14 May

500	Singing duets	£72/166
501	Introduction to computers and software applications	£72/166
502	Drawing for the terrified: part 2	£72/166
503	Wonderful water	£72/166
504	Découpage	£72/166
505	Patchwork and quilting: C&G 7802	£72/166
506	Stumpwork embroidery: C&G 7802	£72/166
507	Machine embroidery: C&G 7802	£72/166

Missenden Abbey *Great Missenden*
ARCA

| **May** | *Time to Learn* | **May** |

12–14 May
508	Blackwork	£AFD
509	Wines of Spain and Portugal	£AFD
510	Painting with pencils	£AFD
511	Enjoying chamber music	£AFD

The Old Rectory *Fittleworth*
ARCA

12–14 May
512	The exercise experience	£AFD
513	Organic gardening	£AFD
514	Machine knitting	£AFD

Pendrell Hall College *Staffs*
ARCA

12–14 May
515	Sebastian Faulks' French trilogy	£80/129
516	The building stones of England	£80/129
517	Ancient Malta	£80/129
518	Spain: dictatorship to democracy	£80/129

Univ Cambridge *Madingley, Cambridge*

12–14 May
| 519 | The spring migration | £100 |

Univ Nottingham *Gibraltar Point*
| 520 | Medieval Lincoln | £145 |

Univ Nottingham *Lincoln*
| 521 | London's River Police 1798–1998 | £170 |

Univ Nottingham *London*

12–14 May
522	Cane and rush seating	£AFD
523	Machine knitting workshop	£AFD
524	Calligraphy: advanced	£AFD

Urchfont Manor College *Devizes*
ARCA

12–14 May
| 525 | The green man | £99 |
| 526 | Workshop for jazz singers | £95 |

Wansfell College *Theydon Bois*
ARCA

12–14 May
| 527 | Utopias: 11th annual Raymond Williams weekend | £70 |

Wedgwood Memorial College *Barlaston*
ARCA

12–14 May
| 528 | Birdwatching in Norfolk and Suffolk | £70/105 |
| 529 | Watercolour landscapes for beginners | £70/105 |

Wensum Lodge *Norwich*
ARCA

12–14 May
530	Silk painting for beginners	£AFD
531	Tassel making and cordspinning	£AFD
532	Willow weaving	£AFD
533	Painting with Turner (with lectures)	£AFD
534	Making the most of your greenhouse	£AFD
535	Jewellery making	£AFD
536	Wood engraving	£AFD

West Dean College *Chichester*
ARCA

12–19 May
| 537 | French language school | £AFD |

Lancashire College *Chorley*
ARCA

13–14 May
| 538 | Gourmet cookery | £AFD |

Acorn Activities *Bournemouth*
539	Interior design	£AFD
540	Decorative interiors and paint effects	£AFD
541	Wood carving	£AFD

Acorn Activities *Herefordshire*
542	Pottery	£AFD
543	IT & the internet	£AFD
544	Garden design	£AFD

Acorn Activities *Scotland*

Time to Learn — May

13–14 May
545 Casal Guidi embroidery   £83
Burton Manor College *Neston, Cheshire*
ARCA

13–15 May
546 Devon on a bike   £99
HF Holidays *Thurlestone Sands*

13–20 May
547 Spring birds of the coast, woods and valleys   £218/280
Field Studies Council *Dale Fort Centre, Pembrokeshire*

13–20 May
548 Landscape painting   £409
HF Holidays *Glen Coe*
549 Landscape painting   £429
HF Holidays *Malhamdale*

14–17 May
550 Mounting and framing pictures – part 1   £AFD
West Dean College *Chichester*
ARCA

14–19 May
551 Stained glass for beginners   £AFD
Higham Hall *Cockermouth*
ARCA

14–19 May
552 The dry painting possibilities of pastels   £AFD
553 Creative watercolour   £AFD
West Dean College *Chichester*
ARCA

14–20 May
554 Watercolour week   £439
Watercolour Weeks at Weobley *Weobley, Hereford*

15–19 May
555 Focus on fitness   £189
HF Holidays *Thurlestone Sands*

16–18 May
556 Painting on china   £AFD
Pendrell Hall College *Staffs*
ARCA

19–21 May
557 Elgar weekend: his life and music   £AFD
Acorn Activities *Herefordshire*
558 Charles Rennie Mackintosh: his life and designs   £AFD
Acorn Activities *Scotland*

19–21 May
559 Trouser fitting   £95
560 Tai Chi   £90
561 What makes a best seller?   £90
Alston Hall College *Preston*
ARCA

19–21 May
562 Art history and appreciation   £78/98
563 Explore pastels with watercolour   £78/98
Belstead House *Ipswich*
ARCA

19–21 May
564 Light orchestra   £106/126
565 Conducting   £106/126
Benslow Music Trust *Hitchin*
ARCA

19–21 May
566 Ballroom dancing   £110
Burton Manor College *Neston, Cheshire*
ARCA

May   *Time to Learn*   May

19-21 May

567	The archaeology of Cranborne Chase	£120/150

Dillington House *Ilminster*
ARCA

19-21 May

568	Using your sketchbook	£158
569	Composition and landscape painting	£158
570	Care and restoration of antique furniture	£158
571	Line dancing for all	£158
572	Bird songs, calls and behaviour	£168
573	Speak Spanish – advanced	£158
574	Using MS Access	£188

The Earnley Concourse *Chichester, Sussex*

19-21 May

575	Rock climbing	£98/125
576	Spring flowers	£87/112

Field Studies Council *Castle Head Centre, Lake District*

19-21 May

577	Bedding and container gardening	£89/114
578	Microscopy for beekeepers	£89/114
579	Watercolour for near beginners	£89/114
580	Spring walking weekend: exploring woodlands and shorelines	£89/114
581	Introduction to wildlife sound recording	£89/114

Field Studies Council *Flatford Mill, Essex*

19-21 May

582	Exploring the world of insects	£89/114
583	Look out for mammals: an identification workshop	£AFD
584	The natural history of the garden	£89/114
585	Watercolours for absolute beginners	£89/114

Field Studies Council *Juniper Hall Centre, Dorking, Surrey*

19-21 May

586	Flower painting	£85/115
587	Hoverfly identification workshop	£90/120
588	The badger	£85/115

Field Studies Council *Preston Montford, Shropshire*

19-21 May

589	Sphagnum weekend	£114/136

Field Studies Council *Rhyd-y-creuau Centre, Snowdonia*

19-21 May

590	Free your voice	£133/155

Hawkwood College *Stroud, Glos*
ARCA

19-21 May

591	Flower painting	£AFD
592	Fabric boxes	£AFD
593	Claudio Monteverdi – an introduction	£AFD

Higham Hall *Cockermouth*
ARCA

19-21 May

594	Singers' weekend	£105*

Jackdaws Educational Trust *Frome, Somerset*
**food included. B & B extra*

19-21 May

595	Sex, lies and clay tablets: the Bronze Age	£107
596	Croquet	£107
597	Graphology (advanced)	£107
598	Drawing for watercolours	£107

Knuston Hall *Irchester*
ARCA

19-21 May

599	Stained glass for beginners and improvers	£AFD
600	Feng Shui	£AFD
601	The pension maze explained	£AFD
602	Build a Website	£AFD
603	Greek	£AFD

Lancashire College *Chorley*
ARCA

19-21 May

604	Make a Japanese quilted bag	£89/115
605	Vaughan Williams to Benjamin Britten	£89/115

Maryland College *Woburn*
ARCA

19-21 May

606	Tai Ji Quan & Chinese health arts	£72/166
607	Writing magazine articles	£72/166
608	Patchwork and quilting: C&G 7900	£72/166
609	Embroidery: C&G 7900 – part two	£72/166
610	Textile decorative techniques: C&G 7802	£72/166
611	Bead needle weaving: C&G 7802 (beginners)	£72/166

Missenden Abbey *Great Missenden*
ARCA

19-21 May

612	Introduction to desk top publishing	£AFD
613	Archaeology of the Adur valley	£AFD
614	Painting – wet in wet	£AFD
615	Harpsichord workshop	£AFD

The Old Rectory *Fittleworth*
ARCA

19-21 May

616	Native American necklaces	£AFD
617	Local history	£AFD
618	Jewellery/silversmithing	£AFD

Pendrell Hall College *Staffs*
ARCA

19-21 May

619	One hundred years ago: a survey of music composed around the turn of the last century	£80/129
620	English Renaissance funerary monuments	£80/129
621	Deciphering Latin inscriptions	£80/129
622	Shakespeare and jealousy	£80/129

Univ Cambridge *Madingley, Cambridge*

19-21 May

623	The English gentleman and his country estates	£99
624	King Priam and the cunning little vixen	£89
625	Painting miniatures and silhouettes	£89

Wansfell College *Theydon Bois*
ARCA

19-21 May

626	SATEB – Esperanto weekend	£70
627	Between the lines – poetry writing	£78

Wedgwood Memorial College *Barlaston*
ARCA

19-21 May

628	Bookbinding – repairing leather bindings	£AFD
629	Low relief and chip carving in wood	£AFD
630	Silversmithing – hammerwork	£AFD
631	Watercolour for beginners	£AFD
632	Woodcarving for beginners	£AFD

West Dean College *Chichester*
ARCA

19-22 May

633	Wine appreciation	£179

HF Holidays *Thurlestone Sands*

19-23 May

634	Islands, birds and boating	£148/190

Field Studies Council *Dale Fort Centre, Pembrokeshire*

19-26 May

635	Nature photography in spring	£230/295

Field Studies Council *Blencathra, Lake District*

20-21 May

636	Mosaics	£AFD
637	Drawing for the terrified	£AFD

Acorn Activities *Herefordshire*

638	Stained glass	£AFD

Acorn Activities *Shropshire*

639	Garden design	£AFD

Acorn Activities *Worcestershire*

20-24 May

640	Parchment craft	£204

HF Holidays *Conwy*

641	Monarch and laureate	£239

HF Holidays *Freshwater Bay*

642	Singing for pleasure	£234
643	Electronic keyboards – intermediate	£249

HF Holidays *Malhamdale*

644	Landscape painting	£249

HF Holidays *Whitby*

20-27 May

645	Sussex walks of discovery	£439

HF Holidays *Abingworth*

646	Painting seascapes	£379

HF Holidays *Freshwater Bay*

647	Square dancing – level 2	£369

HF Holidays *Haytor, Devon*

648	Landscape painting	£374

HF Holidays *Isle of Arran*

649	Landscape painting	£419

HF Holidays *Sedbergh*

20-27 May

650	Birds and plants on the Hebridean island of Islay	£354

Univ Birmingham *Islay*

21-24 May

651	Gardens in spring	£160

Alston Hall College *Preston*
ARCA

21-26 May

652	General silversmithing	£AFD
653	Papermaking from plants	£AFD
654	Cabinet making – part 2	£AFD

West Dean College *Chichester*
ARCA

21-27 May

655	Watercolour week	£439

Watercolour Weeks at Weobley
Weobley, Hereford

22-24 May

656	Golf: from beginner to competitor	£89
657	British art in the C20th	£89

Wansfell College *Theydon Bois*
ARCA

22-25 May

658	Group quartet workshop	£120/145

Benslow Music Trust *Hitchin*
ARCA

Time to Learn

Tuition in
WATERCOLOUR

"The Watercolour Week must be the single most important & productive course for the aspiring watercolourist."

"A course where actual teaching takes place and excellent teaching too."

"Weobley has reinforced my belief that techniques should be taught formally and not just discovered by accident. It is just what I wanted. I wish I had come years ago!"

"Thank you for a wonderful week of intensive watercolour tuition. I cannot imagine anywhere to compare with your methods and inexhaustible patience."

"The questioning of entrenched ideas and the inventiveness of solutions really appealed to me! It has given me the new start I was looking for!"

At Weobley, we are proud to receive regularly, letters like the examples published here. Weobley courses have helped many painters to find new levels of achievement. They provide a wealth of, often neglected, information for the experienced painter and are, at the same time, a valuable introduction to watercolour for the beginner

Weobley Art Centre, The Old Corner House, Broad Street, Weobley, Herefordshire HR4 8SA Tel/Fax 01544 318548
e-mail: enquiries@weobley.demon.co.uk

MISSENDEN ABBEY
your FIRST CHOICE for WEEKENDS and SUMMER SCHOOLS

FIRST CLASS ACCOMMODATION – luxury study bedrooms all with private bathroom – dining rooms, library and garden room with ornate plaster work and ash panelling, a licensed bar, fitness facilities and a peaceful listed garden.

FIRST CLASS TUITION – Nationally acclaimed tutors provide courses in photography, writing, health, art, crafts and humanities. They offer exciting themes, new insights and the groundwork and inspiration to carry on where the course leaves off. Beginners and specialists alike find themselves working to the highest standards and enjoying every minute!

Easily accessible – M1 – M25 (15 mins).
British Rail – Marylebone (40 mins).

Full course information on Internet – http://www.aredu.org.uk/missendenabbey
Missenden Abbey, Chilterns Continuing Education,
The Misbourne School, Great Missenden
Bucks HP16 0BN Tel: 01494 862904

Buckinghamshire County Council

May — Time to Learn — May

22–26 May
659 Painting and drawing from nature £220
Edinburgh College of Art *Benmore, Argyll*

22–26 May
660 Belly dancing £214
HF Holidays *Conistonwater*
661 Photography tour £224
HF Holidays *Thurlestone Sands*

22–26 May
662 Poetry for pleasure £AFD
663 More walks on the wild side £AFD
664 Landscape in watercolour £AFD
The Old Rectory *Fittleworth*
ARCA

24–27 May
665 Singing for beginners £154
HF Holidays *Conwy*
666 Nature and plant photography £179
HF Holidays *Freshwater Bay*

24–31 May
667 Mosses and liverworts £218/280
Field Studies Council *Orielton Centre, Pembrokeshire*

25–29 May
668 Italian opera £105*
Jackdaws Educational Trust *Frome, Somerset*
*food included. B & B extra

26–28 May
669 Christian Arts Conference £75
Ammerdown Centre *Radstock, Bath*

26–28 May
670 Bead needleweaving £78/98
671 Wind ensembles £78/98
Belstead House *Ipswich*
ARCA

26–28 May
672 The intermediate cellist £101/121
673 Voices and viols £106/126
Benslow Music Trust *Hitchin*
ARCA

26–28 May
674 Make a movie £110
675 Handpainted furniture £110
676 Flamenco dancing £109
Burton Manor College *Neston, Cheshire*
ARCA

26–28 May
677 Speak French – advanced £158
678 Using MS Word – level 1 £188
The Earnley Concourse *Chichester, Sussex*

26–28 May
679 Creative embroidery £107
680 Writing your life story £107
Knuston Hall *Irchester*
ARCA

26–28 May
681 Life drawing and painting £89/115
682 Two modern novels: *Amsterdam* and *Crusoe's Daughter* £89/115
Maryland College *Woburn*
ARCA

26–28 May
683 Sketching and walking £AFD
684 Silk painting £AFD
685 The Great Exhibition and the Crystal Palace £AFD
686 Write your autobiography £AFD
The Old Rectory *Fittleworth*
ARCA

26–28 May
687 Stuart parliaments £80/129
688 From the fury of the northmen deliver us £80/129
689 Sisters of the British £80/129
Univ Cambridge *Madingley, Cambridge*

26–28 May
690 Roman archaeology of south east England £AFD
Urchfont Manor College *Devizes*
ARCA

26–28 May
691 3D découpage cards and pictures £89
692 American Indian art and culture £89
693 Italian – advanced £89
Wansfell College *Theydon Bois*
ARCA

26–29 May
694 Jane Austen country £244
The Earnley Concourse *Chichester, Sussex*

26–29 May
695 Lakeland inspired writers and writings £112/144
Field Studies Council *Castle Head Centre, Lake District*

26–29 May
696 Environment for fun: the world beyond our senses £AFD
Field Studies Council *Rhyd-y-creuau Centre, Snowdonia*

26–29 May
697 Wild flowers in early summer £116/150
Field Studies Council *Slapton Ley Centre, Devon*

26–29 May
698 Horse riding £219
HF Holidays *Thurlestone Sands*

26–29 May
699 Spring bridge £AFD
Higham Hall *Cockermouth*
ARCA

26–29 May
700 Gardens around Windsor £290
Univ Nottingham *Windsor*
701 Bede's world – Northumbria in the age of conversion £300
Univ Nottingham *Newton Aycliffe*

26–30 May
702 Paint in your favourite medium £180
703 Tiffany lampshade making £180
Alston Hall College *Preston*
ARCA

26–30 May
704 Birds – sight and sound in early summer £129/172
Field Studies Council *Preston Montford, Shropshire*

26–30 May
705 Landscape painting and drawing: spring coastal colours £125/160
Field Studies Council *Slapton Ley Centre, Devon*

26 May–2 June
706 Landscape painting: watercolours £408
707 Painting on silk: summer workshop £408
The Earnley Concourse *Chichester, Sussex*

26 May–2 June
708 Walking from west to east £230/295
Field Studies Council *Blencathra, Lake District*

26 May–2 June
709 Butterflies and moths £221/283
Field Studies Council *Castle Head Centre, Lake District*

26 May–2 June
710 Woodland biodiversity week £233/290
Field Studies Council *Nettlecombe Court Centre, Exmoor*

26 May–2 June
711 Discovering Shropshire £180/270
712 Landscape painting in watercolour £180/285
Field Studies Council *Preston Montford, Shropshire*

26 May–2 June
713 Spring birds of Snowdonia, Anglesey and the north Wales coast £203/280
Field Studies Council *Rhyd-y-creuau Centre, Snowdonia*

26 May–3 June
714 The Ribble Way £347
**Alston Hall College *Preston*
ARCA**

27–30 May
715 Vibrant voice £179
HF Holidays *Sedbergh*

27–31 May
716 Music making and walking £244
HF Holidays *Whitby*

27 May–1 June
717 Woodwind and brass playing £244
HF Holidays *Whitby*

27 May–3 June
718 Interlude on Lundy: pirates, birds and landscapes in the Bristol channel £740
Field Studies Council Overseas *Lundy Island*

27 May–3 June
719 Birdwatching £399
HF Holidays *Alnmouth*
720 Landscape painting £409
HF Holidays *Conwy*
721 Classical music and walking £364
722 Fossil hunting £374
HF Holidays *Freshwater Bay*
723 The great Scottish waterways £419
HF Holidays *Glen Coe*
724 All sides of Dartmoor £444
HF Holidays *Haytor, Devon*
725 Music making and walking £419
726 Woodwind and brass playing £419
HF Holidays *Whitby*

28 May–1 June
727 Making jewellery using decorative surfaces £AFD
**West Dean College *Chichester*
ARCA**

ART AND CRAFT COURSES IN WEST SUSSEX

Enjoy a stimulating break in idyllic surroundings at our well-equipped centre just a few miles south of Chichester. Weekend, midweek and week long courses open to anyone over the age of 16. Subjects include: *Drawing for Beginners, Life Drawing & Portraits, Watercolours, Landscapes, Print Making, Calligraphy, Chinese Brush Painting, Painting on Silk, Batik, Working Wood, Stained Glass, Picture Framing, Weaving & Embroidery and much more.*

Hotel standard accommodation, good food and excellent leisure facilities. Contact us today for a copy of our latest brochure.

THE EARNLEY CONCOURSE

Earnley, Chichester, West Sussex, PO20 7JL
Tel: (01243) 670392 - Fax: (01243) 670832
Email: info@earnley.co.uk
www.earnley.co.uk

Time to Learn

28 May–2 June
728 Painting – find your psyche £AFD
729 Creative blacksmithing £AFD
730 Woodturning £AFD
West Dean College *Chichester*
ARCA

29 May–2 June
731 Celtic saints of the south west £195
Ammerdown Centre *Radstock, Bath*

29 May–2 June
732 Landscape photography £160/200
Field Studies Council *Blencathra, Lake District*

29 May–2 June
733 Wild flowers £180/230
Field Studies Council *Preston Montford, Shropshire*

29 May–2 June
734 Arctic alpines of Snowdonia £148/192
Field Studies Council *Rhyd-y-creuau Centre, Snowdonia*

29 May–2 June
735 Introducing microfungi £140/180
Field Studies Council *Slapton Ley Centre, Devon*

29 May–2 June
736 Painting boats and harbours £209
HF Holidays *Thurlestone Sands*

29 May–3 June
737 Wet into wet £AFD
738 People sketching £AFD
Higham Hall *Cockermouth*
ARCA

30 May–1 June
739 Discovering modern London 1940–99 £99
740 Shakespeare and his world £89
Wansfell College *Theydon Bois*
ARCA

30 May–2 June
741 Watercolour painting £135
Alston Hall College *Preston*
ARCA

30 May–2 June
742 Introduction to art and drawing £162
Burton Manor College *Neston, Cheshire*
ARCA

30 May–2 June
743 Woodcarving £AFD
744 Discovering Lincolnshire £AFD
Horncastle College *Horncastle*
ARCA

30 May–2 June
745 Conservation and nature reserves £165
Univ Nottingham *Horncastle*

30 May–2 June
746 Practical painting £134
Wansfell College *Theydon Bois*
ARCA

30 May–2 June
747 Printerly painting – painterly printing £160
Wedgwood Memorial College *Barlaston*
ARCA

30 May–3 June
748 Map and compass £253
HF Holidays *Brecon*
749 Get into drama £259
HF Holidays *Sedbergh*

| May | Time to Learn | June |

31 May–2 June
750 Pembrokeshire Coast
  National Park £218/280
Field Studies Council Dale Fort Centre, Pembrokeshire

31 May–2 June
751 Taking your soul to work £AFD
**Hawkwood College Stroud, Glos
ARCA**

31 May–2 June
752 Family learning break £AFD
**Lancashire College Chorley
ARCA**

31 May–3 June
753 Yorkshire on a bike £179
HF Holidays Whitby

June 2000

June
754 Pottery and print making: basics and beginnings in Summer Wineland £AFD
Lindsey-Ward Print-Making and Ceramics Holmfirth, West Yorkshire

1–4 June
755 Arts and crafts in the Lake District £AFD
Univ Birmingham Windermere

1–30 June
756 Russian – individual tuition* £AFD
757 French – individual tuition* £AFD
758 Beginners' Welsh – individual tuition* £AFD
Meirionnydd Languages Trawsfynydd, Gwynedd
*£50 per day, subject to availability. Reduced fees for groups of 2/3 people

2–4 June
759 Ruskin lacemaking £90
760 Piano workshop £90
**Alston Hall College Preston
ARCA**

2–4 June
761 The abolition of war (led by Bruce Kent) £75
Ammerdown Centre Radstock, Bath

2–4 June
762 Playford dance £78/98
**Belstead House Ipswich
ARCA**

2–4 June
763 Wind chamber music £101/121
**Benslow Music Trust Hitchin
ARCA**

2–4 June
764 Bridge for absolute beginners £111
**Burton Manor College Neston, Cheshire
ARCA**

Time to Learn

2–4 June

765	Learn to swim	£158
766	Bridge for beginners: level 1	£158
767	You can write for publication	£158
768	Entertaining with ease	£158
769	Introduction to digital photography	£188

The Earnley Concourse *Chichester, Sussex*

2–4 June

770	Borrowdale's rainforest	£85/115

Field Studies Council *Blencathra, Lake District*

2–4 June

771	Discovering Morecambe Bay	£87/112

Field Studies Council *Castle Head Centre, Lake District*

2–4 June

772	Camera skills 3: introducing nature photography	£92/117
773	Wild flowers for beginners: the top 20 flower families	£89/114
774	Drawing and sketching with watercolour	£89/114

Field Studies Council *Flatford Mill, Essex*

2–4 June

775	Introduction to the smaller diptera	£97/124

Field Studies Council *Juniper Hall Centre, Dorking, Surrey*

2–4 June

776	Stoneworts	£101/130
777	Sedges have edges	£101/130
778	Look out for mammals: an identification workshop	£69/112
779	Birdwatching in the Dales	£86/110

Field Studies Council *Malham Tarn Field Centre, North Yorkshire*

2–4 June

780	Newts	£85/115
781	Birdsong	£85/115
782	Lichens: an introduction	£85/115

Field Studies Council *Preston Montford, Shropshire*

2–4 June

783	Working and playing with nature spirits	£AFD
784	Colour and design through feltmaking	£AFD
785	Meditation to quieten the mind	£96/130

Hawkwood College *Stroud, Glos*
ARCA

2–4 June

786	Diaries from distant lands	£AFD

Horncastle College *Horncastle*
ARCA

2–4 June

787	Discover your voice	£105*

Jackdaws Educational Trust *Frome, Somerset*
*food included. B & B extra

2–4 June

788	Beckett the playwright	£AFD
789	Special clothes making	£107

Knuston Hall *Irchester*
ARCA

2–4 June

790	Interior design for beginners	£AFD
791	France actuelle	£AFD

Lancashire College *Chorley*
ARCA

2–4 June

792	Ireland: the Tudor impact	£89/115
793	Bridge – intermediate	£99/125

Maryland College *Woburn*
ARCA

2–4 June

794	The song recital	£72/166
795	Living joyfully	£72/166
796	Writing for film	£72/166
797	Decoration and colour in calligraphy	£72/166
798	Watercolour and gouache in landscape and garden	£72/166
799	Summer flowers using wet-into-wet techniques	£72/166
800	Portraits	£72/166
801	Crewelwork embroidery	£72/166
802	Upholstery workshop	£72/166
803	Woodcarving: C&G 7802 and 7900	
804	The black and white darkroom: an introduction	£72/166

Missenden Abbey *Great Missenden*
ARCA

2–4 June

805	Chinese brush painting	£AFD
806	Doll's house miniatures (cold porcelain)	£AFD
807	French for holidays	£AFD

Pendrell Hall College *Staffs*
ARCA

2–4 June

808	French weekend	£80/129
809	Wild flowers of East Anglia	£80/129
810	Botanical illustration: pen and ink techniques	£80/129
811	Ecological culture and cultural ecologies	£80/129

Univ Cambridge *Madingley, Cambridge*

2–4 June

812	Diaries from distant places: from Easter Island to Salisbury Plain	£105

Univ Nottingham *Horncastle*

813	Follies and mad hatters: curiosities and eccentricities of England	£155

Univ Nottingham *Bradford upon Avon*

814	Beckett the playwright	£115

Univ Nottingham *Knuston Hall, Wellingborough*

2–4 June

815	Philosophy: Plato's Protagoras	£AFD
816	Making teddy bears	£AFD
817	Audiovisual presentations	£AFD

Urchfont Manor College *Devizes*
ARCA

2–4 June

818	Evolution of residential architecture after the Great Fire	£99

Wansfell College *Theydon Bois*
ARCA

2–4 June

819	The stillness of still life (painting)	£78
820	Auschwitz: exploration of the Holocaust	£78

Wedgwood Memorial College *Barlaston*
ARCA

June — Time to Learn

2–4 June
821	The Flying Dutchman meets *Peter Grimes*	£70/105
822	The parish churches of Norwich	£70/105

Wensum Lodge *Norwich*
ARCA

2–4 June
823	Drawing with charcoal	£AFD
824	Basic blacksmithing	£AFD
825	Batik – creative design	£AFD
826	Hand embroidery	£AFD
827	Walling in flint and stone	£AFD
828	The basics of watercolour painting	£AFD

West Dean College *Chichester*
ARCA

2–5 June
829	Willow figurines and animal structures	£135/175
830	Identifying spring wild flowers	£110/140
831	Artists' workshop	£85/115

Field Studies Council *Blencathra, Lake District*

2–5 June
832	Nature photography in Pembrokeshire	£117/150

Field Studies Council *Dale Fort Centre, Pembrokeshire*

2–5 June
833	Woodland plants	£145/190

Field Studies Council *Preston Montford, Shropshire*

2–5 June
834	Introduction to aromatherapy	£144

HF Holidays *Thurlestone Sands*

2–6 June
835	Paper marbling	£AFD

West Dean College *Chichester*
ARCA

2–9 June
836	Watercolour painting: harbourside views	£408
837	Painting and sketching in the countryside	£408

The Earnley Concourse *Chichester, Sussex*

2–9 June
838	In search of the picturesque	£222/285

Field Studies Council *Juniper Hall Centre, Dorking, Surrey*

2–9 June
839	Doll's house summer school	£AFD
840	Fittleworth singers summer school	£AFD
841	Sketching and painting	£AFD

The Old Rectory *Fittleworth*
ARCA

3–4 June
842	Silversmithing	£AFD
843	Pottery	£AFD

Acorn Activities *Herefordshire*

3–4 June
844	Bookbinding	£65

Alston Hall College *Preston*
ARCA

3–10 June
845	Birdwatching	£399

HF Holidays *Alnmouth*
846	Wildlife of Devon	£454

HF Holidays *Haytor, Devon*
847	Classical music and walking	£389

HF Holidays *Pitlochry*
848	Flat green bowls – improvers	£359

HF Holidays *Selworthy*

June — Time to Learn

3–10 June
849 Painting – an artistic journey through the Lakes £AFD
Higham Hall Cockermouth ARCA

4–7 June
850 Dyeing, discharge and devorée on velvet £AFD
851 Features in raised embroidery £AFD
West Dean College Chichester ARCA

4–9 June
852 Orkney landscape painting £220
Edinburgh College of Art Orkney

4–9 June
853 Handmade books – lettering and binding £AFD
854 The basics of watercolour landscape £AFD
West Dean College Chichester ARCA

4–10 June
855 Lakeland birds £AFD
Higham Hall Cockermouth ARCA

4–10 June
856 Painting the castles of Hereford £439
Watercolour Weeks at Weobley Weobley, Hereford

5–7 June
857 Painting in miniature £110
Burton Manor College Neston, Cheshire ARCA

5–8 June
858 Positive ageing £110
Ammerdown Centre Radstock, Bath

5–9 June
859 Watercolour painting £145
860 Short stories, articles and poetry £145
Ammerdown Centre Radstock, Bath

5–9 June
861 Spring nature photography £187/240
Field Studies Council Juniper Hall Centre, Dorking, Surrey

5–9 June
862 Castles and abbeys of north Yorkshire £350
Univ Birmingham Ripon

5–9 June
863 Literature of Erich Maria Remarque £179
Wansfell College Theydon Bois ARCA

6–9 June
864 Printmaking workshop – colour printing £AFD
West Dean College Chichester ARCA

7–9 June
865 Gardening – the mixed border £AFD
West Dean College Chichester ARCA

7–10 June
866 Landscape painting £169
HF Holidays Derwentwater

7–11 June
867 BSL stage II module 2 £AFD
Lancashire College Chorley ARCA

Time to Learn

UNIVERSITY OF CAMBRIDGE

Board of Continuing Education

SHORT RESIDENTIAL COURSES

Choose from over 100 subjects a year including literature, music, local and national history, ancient Greek, Latin, art history, natural history ... all in 16th century Madingley Hall, set in seven acres of garden. Courses are open to anyone over 18 - there are no academic requirements for admission. Fees are around £129 for a weekend (tuition, single room with en-suite facilities and full-board from Friday dinner to Sunday lunch). Or try one of our **Summer Schools**, our **Day and Evening Classes**, our **Certificate Courses** or our **Study Tours**.

For FREE-brochures please phone, write or fax to :
The Courses Registrar (Ref TTL), University of Cambridge, Board of Continuing Education, Madingley Hall, Madingley, Cambridge CB3 8AQ.
Telephone (01954) 280399.
Fax (01954) 280200.

The University of Cambridge aims to achieve the highest quality in teaching and research

June — Time to Learn — June

7–17 June
868 Orkney: archaeology and wildlife of a living landscape £1100
Field Studies Council Overseas *Orkney*

9–11 June
869 Folk dancing weekend £90
870 Walking stick making £90
Alston Hall College *Preston*
ARCA

9–11 June
871 Bobbin lace £78/98
Belstead House *Ipswich*
ARCA

9–11 June
872 String chamber music £101/121
Benslow Music Trust *Hitchin*
ARCA

9–11 June
873 Literature – the birth of the English novel £70
Birkbeck College Univ London *London*

9–11 June
874 Croquet for beginners £110
Burton Manor College *Neston, Cheshire*
ARCA

9–11 June
875 Summer walking weekend: exploring Suffolk's countryside £89/114
876 Drawing buildings and landscapes using pastel pencils £89/114
877 Camera and computer skills: digital photography £93/119
878 Grass identification and ecology £93/119
Field Studies Council *Flatford Mill, Essex*

9–11 June
879 A weekend with wild orchids £97/124
880 Improving your watercolour technique £89/114
Field Studies Council *Juniper Hall Centre, Dorking, Surrey*

9–11 June
881 Look out for mammals: an identification workshop £69/112
Field Studies Council *Nettlecombe Court Centre, Exmoor*

9–11 June
882 Sedges £90/120
883 Trees and tree identification in the borderlands £85/115
884 Drawing and painting trees £85/115
Field Studies Council *Preston Montford, Shropshire*

9–11 June
885 Music and literature £AFD
886 Furniture restoration/ light upholstery £AFD
Horncastle College *Horncastle*
ARCA

9–11 June
887 The progressive cellist £105*
Jackdaws Educational Trust *Frome, Somerset*
**food included. B & B extra*

9–11 June
888 World War II £107
889 Mosaic making £AFD
890 Homeopathy £AFD
Knuston Hall *Irchester*
ARCA

June — Time to Learn — June

9–11 June
891	Watercolour landscapes	£AFD
892	Introduction to Reiki	£AFD
893	Internet for beginners	£AFD

Lancashire College *Chorley*
ARCA

9–11 June
894	Walking in Bedfordshire	£89/115
895	Writing for radio	£89/115

Maryland College *Woburn*
ARCA

9–11 June
896	History of opera: Wagner	£72/166
897	Silent witness: the banqueting hall	£72/166
898	Tutankhamun's Egypt	£72/166
899	Bridge: slam bidding	£72/166
900	Watercolour: C&G 7802	£72/166
901	A year in colour: picturing blue	£72/166
902	Botanical painting and drawing	£72/166
903	Honiton lace	£72/166

Missenden Abbey *Great Missenden*
ARCA

9–11 June
904	Make a traditional collector's teddy bear	£AFD
905	An introduction to Danish whitework	£AFD
906	Idle or idyll – the English countryside in life, thought and the arts (1851–1914)	£AFD
907	Watercolour workshop	£AFD

The Old Rectory *Fittleworth*
ARCA

9–11 June
908	Follow-on watercolours	£AFD
909	Improvers' bridge	£AFD
910	Basic computing	£AFD

Pendrell Hall College *Staffs*
ARCA

9–11 June
911	Abbeys of the Fens	£80/129
912	The identification of Britain's native trees	£80/129
913	Rhetoric: the art of practical thought and persuasion	£80/129
914	Images of faith	£80/129

Univ Cambridge *Madingley, Cambridge*

9–11 June
915	Homeopathy	£115
916	Mosaic making	£115

Univ Nottingham *Knuston Hall, Wellingborough*

917	Figures and faces – the art of portraiture	£115

Univ Nottingham *Stoke on Trent*

9–11 June
918	Workshop for singers	£95
919	Computing: beginner's plus	£93

Wansfell College *Theydon Bois*
ARCA

9–11 June
920	Jane Austen and the country house	£78
921	Figures and faces: art of portraiture	£82

Wedgwood Memorial College *Barlaston*
ARCA

9–11 June
922	A weekend with the Brontës	£70/105

Wensum Lodge *Norwich*
ARCA

June   *Time to Learn*   **June**

9–11 June
923	Stained glass	£AFD
924	Pen drawing	£AFD
925	General silversmithing	£AFD
926	Glass engraving for beginners	£AFD
927	Painting miniatures and silhouettes	£AFD
928	Wild flower gardening	£AFD

West Dean College *Chichester* **ARCA**

9–12 June
929	Simply wild flowers	£110/138

Field Studies Council *Nettlecombe Court Centre, Exmoor*

9–13 June
930	Diving the Skomer Marine Reserve and Pembrokeshire islands	£195/250

Field Studies Council *Dale Fort Centre, Pembrokeshire*

9–13 June
931	Mountain and hill drawing and walking	£129/172

Field Studies Council *Preston Montford, Shropshire*

10–11 June
932	Papier maché	£AFD
933	Interior design	£AFD
934	Sculpture	£AFD
935	Flower garden	£AFD
936	Cooking for beginners	£AFD

Acorn Activities *Herefordshire*

937	Stained glass	£AFD

Acorn Activities *Shropshire*

10–11 June
938	Water media techniques	£68/90
939	The story of our language	£68/90
940	Elgar	£68/90

Dillington House *Ilminster* **ARCA**

10–11 June
941	Discovering lichens	£50

Field Studies Council *Epping Forest Centre, Essex*

10–13 June
942	Flat green bowls – improvers	£159

HF Holidays *Pitlochry*

10–14 June
943	Castles and holy sites	£249

HF Holidays *Alnmouth*

944	Belly dancing	£189

HF Holidays *Freshwater Bay*

945	Scrabble® for club players	£234

HF Holidays *Whitby*

10–16 June
946	Fine furniture making – part 3	£AFD

West Dean College *Chichester* **ARCA**

10–17 June
947	Bridge and walking	£369
948	Great little trains of Wales	£449

HF Holidays *Conwy*

949	Landscape painting	£419

HF Holidays *Haytor, Devon*

950	Photography tour	£416

HF Holidays *Isle of Arran*

951	Scottish country dancing – level 2	£379

HF Holidays *St Ives*

10–17 June
952	Creative writing	£AFD
953	Abstract painting	£AFD

Higham Hall *Cockermouth* **ARCA**

11–14 June
954	Pottery – throwing teapots and jugs	£AFD

West Dean College *Chichester* **ARCA**

June — Time to Learn

11–15 June
955 Pottery with other activities £AFD
Acorn Activities *Herefordshire*

11–16 June
956 Caring for furniture £AFD
957 Botanical illustration £AFD
West Dean College *Chichester* **ARCA**

11–17 June
958 Watercolour week £439
Watercolour Weeks at Weobley *Weobley, Hereford*

12–14 June
959 Orchids, dragonflies and summer birds £94
Wansfell College *Theydon Bois* **ARCA**

12–16 June
960 Historical holiday – landscape history – fields and woods £165
961 Stress and spirituality – finding the connections £150
Ammerdown Centre *Radstock, Bath*

12–16 June
962 History – from Rome to Dome. 2000 years of London life, culture and development £AFD
Birkbeck College Univ London *London*

12–16 June
963 Portrait painting £298
964 Chinese brush painting £298
The Earnley Concourse *Chichester, Sussex*

12–16 June
965 Spring wild flowers of Snowdonia and the coast £155/199
Field Studies Council *Rhyd-y-creuau Centre, Snowdonia*

13–14 June
966 Computers don't bite – e-mail and Internet for beginners £AFD
Acorn Activities *Herefordshire*

13–15 June
967 Conscience, our secret core and sanctuary £75
Ammerdown Centre *Radstock, Bath*

13–17 June
968 Landscape painting £239
HF Holidays *Pitlochry*

14–16 June
969 England 1900 £89
Wansfell College *Theydon Bois* **ARCA**

14–17 June
970 Hadrian's Wall £194
HF Holidays *Alnmouth*
971 Orienteering £189
HF Holidays *Freshwater Bay*

15–18 June
972 The medieval March – Shropshire in the C12th £220
Univ Nottingham *Shrewsbury*

16–18 June
973 Wildlife weekend £AFD
Acorn Activities *Pembrokeshire*

16–18 June
974 Rogues, witches and vagabonds – crime and punishment in Stuart Lancashire £95

Wedgwood Memorial College
Barlaston Village, Stoke-on-Trent

Enjoy learning in a comfortable, homely ambience.

Everybody welcome to join our open courses:
Week-ends • Mid-week • Summer Schools
• Linked Tutorial Week-ends • One-day Schools.

Small Group/Seminar & Individual Study opportunities: B&B and Self-catering facility. Very reasonable prices.

The College is close to the famous **Potteries** yet rurally situated with its own Arboretum & Sculpture Garden.

Easy access by M6, or Barlaston Village Station (BR) at the foot of the College's extensive grounds.

For details please contact:
Wedgwood Memorial College, Station Road, Barlaston, Stoke-on-Trent, ST12 9DG
Telephone: (01782) 372105, 373427 Fax: (01782) 372393
E-mail: wedgwood.college@staffordshire.gov.uk
Web-site: http://www.aredu.org.uk/wedgwoodcollege

WEEKEND & SHORT COURSES

Wide-ranging topics
•
Friendly country-house atmosphere
•
Excellent tuition
•
Beautiful setting

Leighton Street, Woburn, MK17 9JD

TEL: 01525 292901
FAX: 01525 290856

Residential and non-residential places available at this delightful college

975	Painting	£90
976	Counselling – level I	£90

Alston Hall College *Preston*
ARCA

16–18 June

977	Joy and sorrow in music	£78/98

Belstead House *Ipswich*
ARCA

16–18 June

978	Classical period piano	£106/126
979	Choral weekend	£106/126

Benslow Music Trust *Hitchin*
ARCA

16–18 June

980	Spinal touch	£110

Burton Manor College *Neston, Cheshire*
ARCA

16–18 June

981	Eternal Egypt – an armchair cruise up the Nile	£90/120
982	An invitation to croquet	£90/120
983	An English country house	£105/135

Dillington House *Ilminster*
ARCA

16–18 June

984	Techniques of watercolour painting	£158
985	Mounting and framing pictures	£158
986	Jazz is for everybody	£158
987	The grand tour: history of art	£158
988	Introduction to the PC	£188

The Earnley Concourse *Chichester, Sussex*

16–18 June

989	Drawing and painting wildlife	£89/114
990	Mid summer birdwatching weekend	£89/114
991	British amphibians and reptiles	£93/119

Field Studies Council *Flatford Mill, Essex*

16–18 June

992	Walking the Greensand Ridges	£89/114
993	Photographing wild flowers	£97/124
994	British Dragonfly Society weekend	£97/124

Field Studies Council *Juniper Hall Centre, Dorking, Surrey*

16–18 June

995	Dragonflies and damselflies	£90/120
996	Look out for mammals: an identification workshop	£69/112
997	Pondweeds	£90/120

Field Studies Council *Preston Montford, Shropshire*

16–18 June

998	Visiting Lincolnshire churches	£AFD

Horncastle College *Horncastle*
ARCA

16–18 June

999	Schubert's piano music	£105*

Jackdaws Educational Trust *Frome, Somerset*
***food included. B & B extra*

16–18 June

1000	Blackwork and Assisi embroidery	£107

Knuston Hall *Irchester*
ARCA

16–18 June
1001	Gold thread embroidery for improvers	£AFD
1002	Keep fit for summer	£AFD
1003	Introduction to PowerPoint for presentations	£AFD

**Lancashire College *Chorley*
ARCA**

16–18 June
1004	North India and Rajasthan	£89/115
1005	The medicinal use of plants	£89/115

**Maryland College *Woburn*
ARCA**

16–18 June
1006	Vienna: city of music	£72/166
1007	The great connector: transport history with an emphasis on railways	£72/166
1008	A brief history of philosophy	£72/166
1009	Life class: the Chinese way. Combination of Chinese brush painting theory with observational drawing from a life model	£72/166
1010	Preparing working designs: C&G 7900	£72/166
1011	Bedfordshire lace	£72/166
1012	Embroidery: C&G 7900 part one	£72/166
1013	Textile decorative techniques: C&G 7802	£72/166

**Missenden Abbey *Great Missenden*
ARCA**

16–18 June
1014	Normans and their legacy	£AFD
1015	Glass painting	£AFD
1016	Spanish	£AFD

**Pendrell Hall College *Staffs*
ARCA**

16–18 June
1017	Creative writing: exploring the short story	£150

Univ Birmingham *Ludlow*

16–18 June
1018	The poetry of Edward Thomas	£80/129
1019	Seashores of East Anglia	£80/129
1020	Medieval stained glass	£80/129
1021	Historical archaeology: an introduction	£80/129

Univ Cambridge *Madingley, Cambridge*

16–18 June
1022	Manchester's heritage	£165

Univ Nottingham *Manchester*

16–18 June
1023	Egyptology	£AFD

**Urchfont Manor College *Devizes*
ARCA**

16–18 June
1024	Tai Chi Ch'uan	£89
1025	Great Victorians	£89
1026	Summer music	£89

**Wansfell College *Theydon Bois*
ARCA**

16–18 June
1027	Circle dance	£76
1028	Der Maulkorb: learning German through literature	£80

**Wedgwood Memorial College *Barlaston*
ARCA**

16–18 June
1029	Get on your bike – cycling weekend	£70/105
1030	Splash – beginners' watercolours	£70/105

**Wensum Lodge *Norwich*
ARCA**

June — Time to Learn

16–18 June

1031	Botanical illustration	£AFD
1032	Cane, willow and rush seating, basketry	£AFD
1033	Calligraphy for complete beginners	£AFD
1034	Propagation for your garden	£AFD
1035	Traditional upholstery	£AFD
1036	Creative watercolour	£AFD

West Dean College *Chichester* **ARCA**

16–19 June

1037	Identifying wetland plants	£113/165

Field Studies Council *Slapton Ley Centre, Devon*

16–19 June

1038	Woodcarving – humans and other animals	£AFD

West Dean College *Chichester* **ARCA**

16–23 June

1039	Sussex sketchbook walks	£408

The Earnley Concourse *Chichester, Sussex*

16–23 June

1040	German language school	£AFD

Lancashire College *Chorley* **ARCA**

16–23 June

1041	Stained glass summer school	£AFD
1042	Embroidery summer school	£AFD
1043	Landscape and seascape painting	£AFD

The Old Rectory *Fittleworth* **ARCA**

17–18 June

1044	Computers don't bite – e-mail and Internet for beginners	£AFD

Acorn Activities *Herefordshire*

1045	Garden design	£AFD

Acorn Activities *Worcestershire*

17–19 June

1046	Garden design weekend	£124

HF Holidays *Conwy*

17–21 June

1047	Manx country steaming: railways, tramways and walking on the Isle of Man	£390

Field Studies Council Overseas *Isle of Man*

17–21 June

1048	Birdwatching	£279

HF Holidays *Abingworth*

1049	Yoga	£234

HF Holidays *Brecon*

17–24 June

1050	Landscape painting	£429

HF Holidays *Bourton-on-the-Water*

1051	Photography tour	£429

HF Holidays *Conistonwater*

1052	Folk dancing and walking	£369

HF Holidays *Freshwater Bay*

1053	Bridge and sightseeing	£399

HF Holidays *Haytor, Devon*

1054	Geology of Arran	£384

HF Holidays *Isle of Arran*

1055	Painting boats and harbours	£429

HF Holidays *St Ives*

17–24 June
1056 Mountains and moorlands: the upland habitats of west Wales £460
1057 The Celtic landscapes of west Wales £460
1058 I do like to be beside the seaside: from coast to castle £460
1059 Country houses and gardens of mid-Wales £460
Summer Academy *Univ Wales, Aberystwyth*

18–20 June
1060 Skeined basketmaking £AFD
West Dean College *Chichester ARCA*

18–23 June
1061 Landscape painting £AFD
Acorn Activities *Lake District*
1062 Scuba diving £AFD
Acorn Activities *Pembrokeshire*

18–23 June
1063 Intermediate traditional upholstery £AFD
1064 Silversmithing £AFD
1065 Portrait painting in oils and other media £AFD
1066 Sculptural modelling for plant containers £AFD
West Dean College *Chichester ARCA*

18–24 June
1067 Moving ahead with watercolour £439
Watercolour Weeks at Weobley *Weobley, Hereford*

18–25 June
1068 Painting and prayer retreat £230
Ammerdown Centre *Radstock, Bath*

19–23 June
1069 Botanical illustration £298
The Earnley Concourse *Chichester, Sussex*

19–23 June
1070 Ballroom dancing – level 1 £179
HF Holidays *Thurlestone Sands*

19–24 June
1071 Welsh National Opera £354
HF Holidays *Conwy*

21–23 June
1072 Lacemaking £111
Knuston Hall *Irchester ARCA*

21–23 June
1073 Gardening – colour in the garden £AFD
West Dean College *Chichester ARCA*

21–24 June
1074 Operetta £179
HF Holidays *Brecon*

21–25 June
1075 The universal language of music £105*
Jackdaws Educational Trust *Frome, Somerset*
*food included. B & B extra

23–24 June
1076 Computers don't bite – e-mail and Internet for beginners £AFD
Acorn Activities *Herefordshire*

23–25 June
1077 Recorder consorts £78/98
Belstead House *Ipswich ARCA*

THE ENGLISH LAKE DISTRICT

HIGHAM HALL

**The Lake District's
Residential College For Adult Education**

Amidst England's Lakeland splendour there sits an elegant country house once described by author Evelyn Waugh as "Very Gothic... with turrets, castellations and a perfectly lovely view across the lake to Skiddaw." Higham Hall now offers a tranquillity uniquely conducive to the array of cultural activities, residential courses and study breaks to which it plays host.

"...a quality Country House experience at a very sensible price."

For a prospectus and more information
phone 017687 76276 or write to:
The Director, Higham Hall College, Bassenthwaite Lake, Cockermouth, Cumbria. CA13 9SH
Website:www.higham-hall.org.uk.

June — *Time to Learn* — **June**

23–25 June

1078	Summer saxes	£101/121
1079	Composition	£101/121
1080	Drawing buildings and simple use of perspective	£AFD

Benslow Music Trust *Hitchin*
ARCA

23–25 June

1081	Watercolour workshop – stage 3	£110
1082	Classical guitar workshop	£121

Burton Manor College *Neston, Cheshire*
ARCA

23–25 June

1083	Mozart piano concertos	£90/120
1084	The importance of being Oscar – the life and loves of Oscar Wilde	£90/120
1085	Anglo-Saxon culture and belief	£107/137

Dillington House *Ilminster*
ARCA

23–25 June

1086	Handspinning: fun with fibres	£158
1087	Bridge for beginners: level 2	£158
1088	Speak German – advanced	£158
1089	Introduction to the Internet	£188

The Earnley Concourse *Chichester, Sussex*

23–25 June

1090	Rock climbing for women	£98/125

Field Studies Council *Castle Head Centre, Lake District*

23–25 June

1091	Suffolk's medieval houses	£89/114
1092	Watercolour for absolute beginners	£89/114

Field Studies Council *Flatford Mill, Essex*

23–25 June

1093	British bats, their ecology and the law	£87/112

Field Studies Council *Slapton Ley Centre, Devon*

23–25 June

1094	Countryside walking	£AFD

Horncastle College *Horncastle*
ARCA

23–25 June

1095	Lacemaking	£107
1096	Wind band	£107

Knuston Hall *Irchester*
ARCA

23–25 June

1097	Computing for absolute beginners	£AFD

Lancashire College *Chorley*
ARCA

23–25 June

1098	Alexander Technique	£89/115
1099	Lacemaking: Beds and Bucks point	£89/115

Maryland College *Woburn*
ARCA

23–25 June

1100	Beethoven's piano music	£72/166
1101	Alexander Technique	£72/166
1102	Writing comedy for television	£72/166
1103	Patchwork and quilting: C&G 7900	£72/166
1104	Embroidery: C&G 7900 part two	£72/166
1105	Pottery and porcelain restoration: C&G 7802	£72/166
1106	Stumpwork embroidery: C&G 7802	£72/166
1107	Bead needle weaving: C&G 7802 (advanced)	£72/166
1108	Machine embroidery: C&G 7802	£72/166
1109	The complete Internet: Internet two	£72/166
1110	Colour prints from slides	£72/166

Missenden Abbey *Great Missenden*
ARCA

23–25 June

1111	Haiku	£AFD
1112	Computers without consternation	£AFD
1113	Stockmarket and investment	£AFD
1114	Painting the Impressionist way	£AFD

The Old Rectory *Fittleworth*
ARCA

23–25 June

1115	Byron	£80/129
1116	The Korean War	£80/129
1117	Plato's republic	£80/129
1118	Advanced palaeography	£80/129

Univ Cambridge *Madingley, Cambridge*

23–25 June

1119	The geology of north Yorkshire	£AFD

Univ Liverpool *Whitby*

23–25 June

1120	Merchants and aristocrats in King's Lynn 1680–1780	£160

Univ Nottingham *King's Lynn*

1121	Lost canals and tramroads of the East Midlands	£140

Univ Nottingham *Nottingham*

1122	Welsh National Opera weekend	£180

Univ Nottingham *Llandudno*

23–25 June

1123	Decorative stained glass	£AFD
1124	Lacemaking	£AFD

Urchfont Manor College *Devizes*
ARCA

23–25 June

1125	America in the 1940s and 1950s	£89
1126	Trollope as miniaturist	£89
1127	Embroidery with crewel wools	£89

Wansfell College *Theydon Bois*
ARCA

23–25 June

1128	Age of revolutions: 1770–1890	£74
1129	The depiction of the nude in C19th and C20th painting in France	£78

Wedgwood Memorial College *Barlaston*
ARCA

23–25 June

1130	Desktop publishing – IT weekend	£70/105
1131	An introduction to antiquarian books	£70/105

Wensum Lodge *Norwich*
ARCA

23–25 June
1132 Painting – exploring colour in the Fauve manner £AFD
1133 Loose leaf gilding on glass £AFD
1134 Stained glass £AFD
1135 Batik on silk £AFD
1136 Calligraphy – painting and gilding a miniature £AFD
1137 Photography – vision and light £AFD
West Dean College *Chichester* **ARCA**

23–26 June
1138 Practical Ayuveda £AFD
1139 Alexander Technique £AFD
Hawkwood College *Stroud, Glos* **ARCA**

23–26 June
1140 Jewellery making £AFD
West Dean College *Chichester* **ARCA**

23–30 June
1141 Music inspired by Greek and Roman mythology £408
1142 Calligraphy summer school £408
1143 Painting and sketching: flowers and gardens £408
The Earnley Concourse *Chichester, Sussex*

23–30 June
1144 Italian language school £AFD
Lancashire College *Chorley* **ARCA**

24–25 June
1145 Rush seating £AFD
1146 Drawing for the terrified £AFD
1147 Gourmet cookery £AFD
Acorn Activities *Herefordshire*
1148 Stained glass £AFD
Acorn Activities *Shropshire*
1149 Dry stone walling £AFD
Acorn Activities *Shropshire/Welsh Border*

1150 Flower garden £AFD
Acorn Activities *Scotland*

24–27 June
1151 Secret gardens of the Lake District £120/160
Field Studies Council *Blencathra, Lake District*

24–27 June
1152 Nature and plant photography £199
HF Holidays *Pitlochry*

24 June–1 July
1153 Painting the early summer landscape £225/290
Field Studies Council *Blencathra, Lake District*

24 June–1 July
1154 Landscape painting £449
HF Holidays *Abingworth*
1155 Landscape painting £439
HF Holidays *Brecon*
1156 Railways in the north-west £444
HF Holidays *Conistonwater*
1157 Birdwatching £419
HF Holidays *Conwy*
1158 Painting flowers and gardens £389
HF Holidays *Dovedale*
1159 Croquet – beginners £359
HF Holidays *Freshwater Bay*
1160 Summer wildlife £374
HF Holidays *Isle of Arran*
1161 Landscape painting £449
1162 Choral singing £409
HF Holidays *Whitby*

24 June–1 July
1163 The rise and fall of King Cotton £460
1164 Wives, daughters and literary sisters £490
Summer Academy *UMIST (Manchester)*

June — Time to Learn — June

1165 Stirling: the hub of
Scottish history £490
Summer Academy *Univ Stirling*

24 June–7 July
1166 Stones and bones: the
archaeology of Scotland £435
Univ Edinburgh *Edinburgh*

25–30 June
1167 Bobbin lacemaking £AFD
Dillington House *Ilminster*
ARCA

25–30 June
1168 Shakespeare in opera £AFD
Higham Hall *Cockermouth*
ARCA

25–30 June
1169 More Wessex walks £AFD
Urchfont Manor College *Devizes*
ARCA

25–30 June
1170 Drawing and painting
landscape £AFD
1171 Adventurous drawing £AFD
West Dean College *Chichester*
ARCA

25 June–1 July
1172 Bobbin lacemaking £AFD
Dillington House *Ilminster*
ARCA

25 June–1 July
1173 Watercolour week £439
Watercolour Weeks at Weobley
Weobley, Hereford

25 June–3 July
1174 Painting £AFD
Higham Hall *Cockermouth*
ARCA

26–28 June
1175 These were the Greeks £89
Wansfell College *Theydon Bois*
ARCA

26–30 June
1176 Jewish Christian summer
school – part 1 £145
Ammerdown Centre *Radstock, Bath*

26–30 June
1177 Better bridge: improve
your card play £298
The Earnley Concourse *Chichester,*
Sussex

26–30 June
1178 English gardens: visits
and lectures £228/300
Maryland College *Woburn*
ARCA

26–30 June
1179 Getting the best from
your camera £AFD
1180 Discovering stone carving
for beginners £AFD
1181 Pottery – coil pots with
slip decoration £AFD
1182 Painting on silk and
velvet £AFD
West Dean College *Chichester*
ARCA

27 June–2 July
1183 Singers and
accompanists £105*
Jackdaws Educational Trust *Frome,*
Somerset
*food included. B & B extra

28–30 June
1184 Woods and fields in mid-
summer £89
Wansfell College *Theydon Bois*
ARCA

The Centre is set within the beauty and peace of Ammerdown Park in Somerset and has a reputation for excellent food and a friendly atmosphere.

Ammerdown offers a wide variety of residential or day courses. Stays possible at other times.

Accommodation is in 30 single, 6 double, and 5 family rooms, self catering facilities also available.

For full programme please contact:

The Ammerdown Centre, Radstock, Bath, BA3 5SW.

Tel:(01761) 433709 Fax: (01761) 433094
e-mail: centre@ammerdown.freeerve.co.uk
http://www.midsomernorton.co.uk/smallpages/ammerdown.htm

THE WORLD LEADER IN SPECIAL INTEREST HOLIDAYS

Over 200 different interests to choose from:

from Alexander Technique to Yoga
•
Crafts to Theatre & Literature
•
Natural History to British Heritage
•
Music Making to Dancing

The choice is endless

Available year round, 2-7 nights, choose from 19 Country House locations

Call for an HF Brochure today.

Tel: 0800 980 1324

Quote ref. FX51
or write to: Dept. FX51, HF Holidays,
Imperial House, Edgware Road,
London NW9 5AL

LANGUAGE COURSES

50 Sheepcote Street, Birmingham, B16 8AJ
Tel: 0121 303 0114 - Fax: 0121 303 4782
E-mail: brasshouse@easynet.co.uk
www.birmingham.gov.uk/brasshouse/

Japanese Residential Weekend

8 - 9 April 2000
Saturday morning 09.30 to Sunday afternoon 16.00
Optional meeting on Friday evening to attend Japan Society meeting.
Price from £103 to £143 with accommodation. Non residential £52

French Course Abroad

1 week course in Brittany - 28 May - 4 June 2000
£452 inclusive of transport, full board accommodation, teaching & excursions

Time to Learn

28 June–1 July
1185 Silk painting £166
HF Holidays *Alnmouth*

29 June–3 July
1186 Roman Scotland £325
Univ Nottingham *Stirling*

30 June–1 July
1187 Using MS Excel £188
The Earnley Concourse *Chichester, Sussex*

30 June–2 July
1188 Drawing for the terrified I £90
1189 Lancashire people through their letters £90
Alston Hall College *Preston*
ARCA

30 June–2 July
1190 Jewish Christian summer school – part 2 £75
1191 Massage and meditation £75
Ammerdown Centre *Radstock, Bath*

30 June–2 July
1192 Patterns and motifs in free machine embroidery £78/98
1193 Painting coastal landscapes £78/98
Belstead House *Ipswich*
ARCA

30 June–2 July
1194 Harpsichord weekend £106/126
Benslow Music Trust *Hitchin*
ARCA

30 June–2 July
1195 Look out for mammals: an identification workshop £69/112
Field Studies Council *Blencathra, Lake District*

30 June–2 July
1196 Identifying plants of freshwater margins £89/114
1197 Identifying bumblebees £89/114
1198 Painting flowers in a Suffolk garden £92/117
1199 New Directions in watercolour £89/114
Field Studies Council *Flatford Mill, Essex*

30 June–2 July
1200 Identifying grasses in flowers £97/124
1201 Painting and drawing butterflies £89/114
Field Studies Council *Juniper Hall Centre, Dorking, Surrey*

30 June–2 July
1202 Silk painting £101/135
Hawkwood College *Stroud, Glos*
ARCA

30 June–2 July
1203 Light and the landscape £AFD
Knuston Hall *Irchester*
ARCA

30 June–2 July
1204 You too can heal and colour therapy £AFD
1205 Databases using MS ACCESS £AFD
1206 Deutschland heute £AFD
Lancashire College *Chorley*
ARCA

30 June–2 July
1207 The making of the English village £89/115
1208 Stained glass: ecclesiastic and secular £89/115
Maryland College *Woburn*
ARCA

30 June–2 July

1209	Mediaeval castles	£72/166
1210	Writing science fiction and fantasy	£72/166
1211	Watercolour: C&G 7802	£72/166
1212	Oil painting	£72/166
1213	Cubism with links to Expressionism	£72/166
1214	Miniature furniture	£72/166
1215	Woodcarving: C&G 7802 and 7900	£72/166

Missenden Abbey *Great Missenden*
ARCA

30 June–2 July

1216	Through the garden gate	£AFD
1217	Digital cameras	£AFD

Pendrell Hall College *Staffs*
ARCA

30 June–2 July

1218	Public parks and gardens	£80/129

Univ Cambridge *Madingley, Cambridge*

30 June–2 July

1219	Art workshop: colours of the countryside	£115

Univ Nottingham *Knuston Hall, Wellingborough*

30 June–2 July

1220	Screen printing and dye painting	£AFD
1221	Choral weekend	£AFD

Urchfont Manor College *Devizes*
ARCA

30 June–2 July

1222	From castle to cottage	£99
1223	Bobbin lacemaking	£89

Wansfell College *Theydon Bois*
ARCA

30 June–2 July

1224	Oscar Wilde – his life and loves	£80
1225	Cézanne	£80

Wedgwood Memorial College *Barlaston*
ARCA

30 June–2 July

1226	Jewellery – gemstones and settings	£AFD
1227	Caring for furniture	£AFD
1228	Basic blacksmithing	£AFD
1229	Pottery – throwing in porcelain	£AFD
1230	Woodturning	£AFD

West Dean College *Chichester*
ARCA

30 June–3 July

1231	Photography tour	£144

HF Holidays *Thurlestone Sands*

30 June–3 July

1232	Light, atmosphere and texture in watercolour	£AFD

West Dean College *Chichester*
ARCA

30 June–7 July

1233	Painting and sketching: boats and ships	£408
1234	Watercolour painting: flowers and gardens	£408
1235	Looking at wildlife	£408
1236	Walking the South Downs Way	£408

The Earnley Concourse *Chichester, Sussex*

30 June–7 July

1237	Painting summer in watercolour and pastels	£AFD
1238	Footloose in Sussex	£AFD
1239	Calligraphy summer school	£AFD

The Old Rectory *Fittleworth*
ARCA

30 June–7 July

1240	Bookbinding	£AFD

West Dean College *Chichester*
ARCA

July 2000

July
1241 Egyptology: the culture of Ancient Egypt – a 3000 year journey £190
1242 The Ancient Egyptians: the bio-anthropological perspective £190
Birkbeck College Univ London *London*

July
1243 Pottery and print making: basics and beginnings in Summer Wineland £AFD
Lindsey-Ward Print-Making and Ceramics *Holmfirth, West Yorkshire*

1–2 July
1244 Pottery £AFD
1245 Silversmithing £AFD
Acorn Activities *Herefordshire*
1246 Stone carving £AFD
Acorn Activities *Powys*
1247 Flower garden £AFD
Acorn Activities *Worcestershire*

1–2 July
1248 Tai Chi £AFD
Pendrell Hall College *Staffs*
ARCA

1–5 July
1249 Literary Yorkshire £279
HF Holidays *Whitby*

1–7 July
1250 Creative writing: short story £215
1251 Scottish literature: Scottish poetry £155
Univ Edinburgh *Edinburgh*

1–8 July
1252 Northumbria walks of discovery £379
HF Holidays *Alnmouth*
1253 Landscape painting £439
HF Holidays *Bourton-on-the-Water*
1254 Improve your swimming £409
HF Holidays *Brecon*
1255 Bridge and sightseeing £369
HF Holidays *Derwentwater*
1256 Landscape painting £374
HF Holidays *Isle of Arran*
1257 Landscape painting £424
HF Holidays *Selworthy*

1–8 July
1258 Landscapes and flowers £AFD
1259 Walking £AFD
Higham Hall *Cockermouth*
ARCA

1–8 July
1260 The story of three cathedrals: Gloucester, Bristol and Wells £490
1261 The novel in English 1880–1914: a world in literature £490
1262 Heaven, earth and man in Chinese art £490
Summer Academy *Univ Bristol*
1263 English customs and traditions £460
1264 Wildflowers of the Peak District £460
1265 Delving into antiques £490
Summer Academy *Univ Sheffield*
1266 The Scottish country house – a place in the landscape £490
Summer Academy *Univ Stirling*

July — Time to Learn — July

1–21 July
1267 Scottish Gaelic:
    elementary   £265
Univ Edinburgh *Edinburgh*

1–31 July
1268 Russian – individual
    tuition*   £AFD
1269 French – individual
    tuition*   £AFD
1270 Beginners' Welsh –
    individual tuition*   £AFD
Meirionnydd Languages *Trawsfynydd, Gwynedd*
*£50 per day, subject to availability. Reduced fees for groups of 2/3 people

2–6 July
1271 Writing summer school –
    1st novel   £180
Alston Hall College *Preston*
ARCA

2–7 July
1272 Portrait summer school   £240
Alston Hall College *Preston*
ARCA

2–7 July
1273 Hardanger – pulled and
    drawn thread work   £107
Knuston Hall *Irchester*
ARCA

2–7 July
1274 Silversmithing and
    jewellery   £AFD
1275 Tassel making, braid
    and fringe weaving   £AFD
1276 Gilding – part 1   £AFD
West Dean College *Chichester*
ARCA

2–8 July
1277 Drawing and watercolour
    for the beginner   £439
Watercolour Weeks at Weobley
Weobley, Hereford

3–6 July
1278 Wind quartet summer
    school   £145/185
Benslow Music Trust *Hitchin*
ARCA

3–7 July
1279 Christian ethics   £75
Ammerdown Centre *Radstock, Bath*

3–7 July
1280 Landscape painting   £213
Burton Manor College *Neston, Cheshire*
ARCA

3–7 July
1281 Wildlife of south Devon   £214
HF Holidays *Thurlestone Sands*

3–7 July
1282 Spanish language
    (post O level)   £156/220
Maryland College *Woburn*
ARCA

3–7 July
1283 Painting   £AFD
Urchfont Manor College *Devizes*
ARCA

3–7 July
1284 Painting and drawing –
    farms   £AFD
West Dean College *Chichester*
ARCA

3–13 July
1285 Scagliola   £AFD
West Dean College *Chichester*
ARCA

3–14 July
1286 Drama: London's plays
    in performance   £360
Birkbeck College Univ London *London*

July   *Time to Learn*   July

5–7 July
1287 More Essex churches   £99
Wansfell College *Theydon Bois*
ARCA

5–8 July
1288 York Mystery Plays   £224
HF Holidays *Whitby*

5–9 July
1289 Tiffany lampshade making £231
Burton Manor College *Neston, Cheshire*
ARCA

5–12 July
1290 Colonsay: wild flowers and fascinations of a Hebridean island   £820
Field Studies Council Overseas *Isle of Colonsay, Scotland*

7–9 July
1291 Elgar weekend: his life and music   £AFD
Acorn Activities *Herefordshire*

7–9 July
1292 Music appreciation   £95
1293 Counselling level I   £90
Alston Hall College *Preston*
ARCA

7–9 July
1294 Silent retreat   £75
Ammerdown Centre *Radstock, Bath*

7–9 July
1295 String chamber music   £126/146
Benslow Music Trust *Hitchin*
ARCA

7–9 July
1296 Feature writing   £110
Burton Manor College *Neston, Cheshire*
ARCA

7–9 July
1297 Introduction to desk top publishing   £188
The Earnley Concourse *Chichester, Sussex*

7–9 July
1298 Botanic medicine   £85/115
Field Studies Council *Blencathra, Lake District*

7–9 July
1299 The romance of windmills   £89/114
1300 Woodland butterflies in south-east England   £89/114
Field Studies Council *Juniper Hall Centre, Dorking, Surrey*

7–9 July
1301 Bedfordshire lace – all levels   £107
1302 Mah Jong for beginners   £107
1303 Flower painting   £107
Knuston Hall *Irchester*
ARCA

7–9 July
1304 The making of medieval Spain   £89/115
1305 A history of the English public house and inn signs   £89/115
Maryland College *Woburn*
ARCA

7–9 July
1306 Landscape painting in oils and acrylics   £AFD
1307 Oriental dancing   £AFD
1308 Raffia craft   £AFD
The Old Rectory *Fittleworth*
ARCA

7–9 July
1309 With Thomas Hardy in Wessex   £185
Univ Birmingham *Blandford Forum*

Birkbeck has an excellent reputation for providing high quality part-time courses for mature students.

Summer Schools

Why not treat yourself to something different this year?

- **DRAMA**
  London's Plays in Performance 3 - 14 July
  A unique opportunity to visit some of the world's finest performances.
  Fees (approx): £360 per week (includes tuition, accommodation & theatre tickets). For full details, please call 020 7631 6674

- **EGYPTOLOGY**
  The Culture of Ancient Egypt: A 3,000 year Journey (July, dates tba)
  The Ancient Egyptians: The Bio-Anthropological Perspective (July, dates tba)
  Fees (approximate): £190 per week (no concessions; non-residential).
  For full details, please call 020 7631 6627.

- **HISTORY**
  From Rome to Dome: 2,000 Years of London Life, Culture & Development 12 - 16 June
  Fees tba (1 week or individual days; non-residential).
  For full details, please call 020 7631 6652.

- **LITERATURE**
  The Birth of the English Novel 9 -11 June
  Fees: £70/£35 concessions (non-residential)
  Victorian Encounters: Publishers, Editors & Readers 20 - 22 July
  Fees: £80/£44 concessions (non-residential).
  For full details, please call 020 7631 6674.

- **WESTONBIRT** 22 July - 5 August
  Take a study break in the country, subjects include: archaeology • art history • botany • creative writing • Egyptology • garden history • history • literature • music • philosophy • psychology
  Fees: £365 per week (choose from 1 or 2 weeks; Gloucestershire based; includes tuition, full board & accommodation).
  For full details, please call 020 7631 6660.

FACULTY OF CONTINUING EDUCATION
Birkbeck College 26 Russell Square London WC1B 5DQ
Telephone 0800 631 6633   Fax 020 7631 6688
email info@bbk.ac.uk   URL http://www.bbk.ac.uk/

Time to Learn — July

7–9 July
1310 Italian weekend £80/129
1311 The great church £80/129
1312 Botanical illustration £80/129
1313 Mackintosh and Wright £80/129
Univ Cambridge *Madingley, Cambridge*

7–9 July
1314 Early Netherlandish art in the time of Jan van Eyck £145
Univ Nottingham *Lucy Cavendish College, Cambridge*
1315 Jane Austen's Hampshire £145
Univ Nottingham *Winchester*

7–9 July
1316 The story of steam £99
1317 Flower and plant illustration in watercolour £89
1318 Workshop for singers £95
Wansfell College *Theydon Bois*
ARCA

7–9 July
1319 Jazz on a summer's weekend £76
1320 Summer walking £76
Wedgwood Memorial College Barlaston
ARCA

7–9 July
1321 Portrait painting – intensive £70/105
1322 Neolithic and Bronze Age Norfolk £70/105
Wensum Lodge *Norwich*
ARCA

7–10 July
1323 Borrowdale's wetlands and wild places £120/160
1324 Mountain flowers £120/160
Field Studies Council *Blencathra, Lake District*

7–10 July
1325 Writing for pleasure £164
HF Holidays *Thurlestone Sands*

7–14 July
1326 Landscape painting £408
1327 Drawing and painting for beginners £408
1328 Looking at country houses £463
The Earnley Concourse *Chichester, Sussex*

8–9 July
1329 Photography £AFD
1330 Cane seating £AFD
Acorn Activities *Herefordshire*
1331 IT and the Internet £AFD
1332 Flower garden £AFD
Acorn Activities *Scotland*
1333 Stained glass £AFD
Acorn Activities *Shropshire*

8–12 July
1334 Discover wild flowers £239
HF Holidays *Freshwater Bay*

8–14 July
1335 Scottish literature: the Scottish novel £155
1336 The geology of southern Scotland £210
1337 Renaissance and Reformation in Scotland £180
1338 Scottish architecture: late mediaeval and Scottish Renaissance £210
Univ Edinburgh *Edinburgh*

8–15 July
1339 Walking with barn dancing £379
HF Holidays *Conistonwater*
1340 Landscape painting £409
HF Holidays *Conwy*
1341 Derbyshire on a bike £354
HF Holidays *Dovedale*

July — Time to Learn

1342 Bridge and sightseeing £439
HF Holidays *Malhamdale*
1343 Railways in the Scottish Highlands £469
HF Holidays *Pitlochry*
1344 Fossil hunting £399
HF Holidays *Selworthy*
1345 York Early Music Festival £479
HF Holidays *Whitby*

8–15 July
1346 Wet on wet £AFD
1347 Recorder week £AFD
Higham Hall *Cockermouth*
ARCA

8–15 July
1348 The growth of the English country house and garden £490
1349 The medieval world: the churches and monasteries of Wessex £490
1350 West Country geology and scenery £490
Summer Academy *Univ Bristol*
1351 Durham Cathedral: monastery and church £460
1352 From Celts to Vikings: ancient kingdoms of the north £460
Summer Academy *Univ Durham*
1353 Architecture and collections of Victorian Manchester £490
1354 From Oldham to Ischia – the life and works of William Walton £460
Summer Academy *UMIST (Manchester)*
1355 The stately homes of Derbyshire £490
1356 The Pre-Raphaelites £460
Summer Academy *Univ Sheffield*
1357 Scotland's struggle for independence £490
Summer Academy *Univ Stirling*
1358 The mystery plays, minster and millennium £490
Summer Academy *Univ York*

8–15 July
1359 Archaeology of the Shetlands £850
Univ Nottingham *Lerwick, Shetland*

8–21 July
1360 Creative writing: playwriting £350
1361 Scottish Gaelic: intermediate/advanced £190
Univ Edinburgh *Edinburgh*

9–13 July
1362 Pottery with other activities £AFD
Acorn Activities *Herefordshire*

9–13 July
1363 Botanical illustration £AFD
Univ Cambridge *Madingley, Cambridge*

9–14 July
1364 Scuba diving £AFD
Acorn Activities *Pembrokeshire*

9–15 July
1365 Great expectations £AFD
Acorn Activities *Somerset*

9–15 July
1366 Pen and ink with watercolour £439
Watercolour Weeks at Weobley *Weobley, Hereford*

10–13 July
1367 The demon drink £144
Wansfell College *Theydon Bois*
ARCA

10–14 July
1368 Scrabble® and walking £189
HF Holidays *Thurlestone Sands*

10–14 July
1369 Visiting the Sussex past £AFD
1370 Upholstery, chair caning
 and seagrass £AFD
1371 Painting Sussex £AFD
The Old Rectory *Fittleworth*
ARCA

10–14 July
1372 The Viking age in England
 and beyond £AFD
Univ Cambridge *Madingley, Cambridge*

10–14 July
1373 Summer course of piano
 and performance £179
Wansfell College *Theydon Bois*
ARCA

10–16 July
1374 International viol
 summer school £280/320
Benslow Music Trust *Hitchin*
ARCA

10–28 July
1375 Portfolio preparation £AFD
1376 Absolute beginners £AFD
1377 General painting £AFD
1378 Life drawing £AFD
1379 Calligraphy £AFD
1380 Tapestry £AFD
1381 Artist masterclasses £AFD
1382 Stone carving £AFD
1383 Sculpture for outdoors £AFD
1384 Life modelling £AFD
1385 Bronze casting £AFD
1386 Web page design £AFD
1387 Computer aided design £AFD
1388 Ceramics £AFD
1389 Film/video £AFD
Edinburgh College of Art *Edinburgh*

13–14 July
1390 Mary Magdalen in
 scripture, art and story £40
Ammerdown Centre *Radstock, Bath*

14–16 July
1391 Rural surprises weekend:
 rural life £AFD
Acorn Activities *Herefordshire*

14–16 July
1392 Early medieval art £95
1393 Honiton lace £90
1394 Antiques £95
Alston Hall College *Preston*
ARCA

14–16 July
1395 Folk singing £78/98
Belstead House *Ipswich*
ARCA

14–16 July
1396 Linen projects £135
Burton Manor College *Neston, Cheshire*
ARCA

14–16 July
1397 Rock scrambling in
 the Lake District £98/125
1398 Ferns and wild flowers
 of carboniferous
 limestone £87/112
Field Studies Council *Castle Head Centre, Lake District*

14–16 July
1399 Identifying dragonflies
 and damselflies £92/117
1400 Camera skills 1:
 making your camera
 work for you £92/117
1401 Watercolour for
 absolute beginners £89/114
Field Studies Council *Flatford Mill, Essex*

Time to Learn

14–16 July

1402	Getting to grips with grasses	£90/120
1403	In search of the red kite and other birds	£85/115

Field Studies Council *Preston Montford, Shropshire*

14–16 July

1404	Chamber music weekend for woodwind and horns	£105*

Jackdaws Educational Trust *Frome, Somerset*
*food included. B & B extra

14–16 July

1405	Embroidery	£107
1406	Wine appreciation	£107
1407	Creative patchwork	£107
1408	Recorders and strings	£107

Knuston Hall *Irchester*
ARCA

14–16 July

1409	Beadwork	£AFD
1410	Writing for pleasure and publication	£AFD
1411	First aid for beginners	£AFD
1412	Men are from Mars, women are from Venus	£AFD
1413	Posters, pics, adverts – graphic illustrations	£AFD

Lancashire College *Chorley*
ARCA

14–16 July

1414	Make the most of your spoken voice	£89/115
1415	Jazz piano greats	£89/115

Maryland College *Woburn*
ARCA

14–16 July

1416	Yoga: relaxation and health	£AFD
1417	Painting roses	£AFD
1418	England's medieval cathedrals	£AFD
1419	A very English enigma: Edward Elgar	£AFD

The Old Rectory *Fittleworth*
ARCA

14–16 July

1420	Recorder playing: technique and ensemble	£156/195

Univ Birmingham *Birmingham*

14–16 July

1421	The late Gothic in England	£80/129

Univ Cambridge *Madingley, Cambridge*

14–16 July

1422	Moths and butterflies	£100

Univ Nottingham *Gibraltar Point*

14–16 July

1423	The hill figures of Wessex	£AFD
1424	More family history	£AFD

Urchfont Manor College *Devizes*
ARCA

14–16 July

1425	Bridge	£89

Wansfell College *Theydon Bois*
ARCA

14–16 July

1426	Watercolour painting weekend	£80
1427	Contemporary poetry: movements/personalities/debate	£76

Wedgwood Memorial College *Barlaston*
ARCA

SPECIAL INTEREST COURSES IN WEST SUSSEX

Enjoy a stimulating break in idyllic surroundings at our well-equipped centre just a few miles south of Chichester. Weekend, midweek and week long courses open to anyone over the age of 16. Subjects include: *Computer Studies, Cookery & Wine Tasting, Wildlife Studies, Health & Fitness, Swimming, Music Making and Musical Appreciation, Historical Studies, Creative Writing, Communication Skills and much more.*

Hotel standard accommodation, good food and excellent leisure facilities. Contact us today for a copy of our latest brochure.

THE EARNLEY CONCOURSE

Earnley, Chichester, West Sussex, PO20 7JL
Tel: (01243) 670392 - Fax: (01243) 670832
Email: info@earnley.co.uk
www.earnley.co.uk

14–16 July
1428 Designing your own furniture — £AFD
1429 Making a holiday sketchbook — £AFD
1430 Painting – water and reflections — £AFD
West Dean College *Chichester* **ARCA**

14–17 July
1431 Deadnettles and figworts: identifying lamiaceae and scrophulariace — £135/190
Field Studies Council *Preston Montford, Shropshire*

14–17 July
1432 Landscape as panorama — £AFD
Univ Cambridge *Madingley, Cambridge*

14–18 July
1433 Great and little trains — £135/195
Field Studies Council *Preston Montford, Shropshire*

14–21 July
1434 Mapping the imagination — £AFD
1435 Film studies — £AFD
Univ Cambridge *Madingley, Cambridge*

15–16 July
1436 Spinning — £AFD
Acorn Activities *Brecon*
1437 Camcorder and video production skills — £AFD
1438 Drawing for the terrified — £AFD
Acorn Activities *Herefordshire*
1439 Dry stone walling — £AFD
Acorn Activities *Shropshire/Welsh Border*

15–19 July
1440 Croquet – players — £244
HF Holidays *Bourton-on-the-Water*

15–21 July
1441 Enlightenment Scotland — £180
1442 Scottish architecture: Scottish classical, Scots baronial and the C20th — £210
1443 Nature conservation in Scotland — £205
1444 Oral presentation skills — £180
Univ Edinburgh *Edinburgh*

15–21 July
1445 The Chilingirian string quartet course — £AFD
West Dean College *Chichester* **ARCA**

15–22 July
1446 Landscape painting — £399
HF Holidays *Alnmouth*
1447 Croquet – players — £409
HF Holidays *Bourton-on-the-Water*
1448 Landscape painting — £444
HF Holidays *Glen Coe*
1449 Photography tour — £489
HF Holidays *Haytor, Devon*

15–22 July
1450 Aristocrats and arrivistes: great families of the north — £460
1451 From Lindisfarne to Bede: early Christian Northumbria — £460
Summer Academy *Univ Durham*
1452 GI airmen – the 8th and 9th USAAF in East Anglia in World War II — £460
1453 Detective work in north Norfolk churches — £460
1454 East Anglia in art, literature and music — £460
Summer Academy *Univ East Anglia, Norwich*
1455 The world of Jane Austen — £460
1456 Rituals, shrines and sacrifice in the Roman south west — £460
1457 Discover Dartmoor's wild plants and animals — £460
Summer Academy *Univ Exeter*

1458 Glass, lakes and steam	£490
1459 Information at your fingertips: the wonders of the World Wide Web	£460

Summer Academy Univ Kent, Canterbury

1460 Medieval stained glass in the Thames valley	£490
1461 The British monarchy in Berkshire and the Thames valley	£490
1462 Humps and bumps: understanding the archaeological landscape	£490
1463 Writing space, writing places	£490

Summer Academy Univ Reading

1464 Roman Britain	£460
1465 In praise of trees	£460
1466 Aromatherapy and massage in theory and practice	£420

Summer Academy Univ Sheffield

1467 Scottish poetry through the ages	£490

Summer Academy Univ Stirling

16–18 July

1468 Buying and drying wood	£AFD

West Dean College Chichester ARCA

16–19 July

1469 Exploring the tarot for fun and insight	£AFD
1470 Brushing away the cobwebs: painting in watercolours	£AFD
1471 Papermaking	£AFD

Dillington House Ilminster ARCA

16–20 July

1472 Embroidered fabric covered boxes	£180
1473 Batik	£190

Alston Hall College Preston ARCA

16–21 July

1474 Summer painting school	£AFD

Pendrell Hall College Staffs ARCA

16–21 July

1475 Graining, marbling and paint techniques	£AFD

West Dean College Chichester ARCA

16–22 July

1476 China restoration	£AFD

Higham Hall Cockermouth ARCA

17–19 July

1477 Magic squares patchwork	£89

Wansfell College Theydon Bois ARCA

17–21 July

1478 Portrait painting	£298
1479 Calligraphy and creative lettering	£298
1480 Stained glass	£298

The Earnley Concourse Chichester, Sussex

17–21 July

1481 National Vegetation Classification: grasslands and woodlands	£200/250

Field Studies Council Preston Montford, Shropshire

17–21 July

1482 Landscape painting	£214

HF Holidays Thurlestone Sands

17–21 July

1483 Summer painting – all media	£156/220

Maryland College Woburn ARCA

July — Time to Learn

17–21 July
1484 How to write good
 fiction £AFD
1485 Mass, weight and
 volume £AFD
Univ Cambridge *Madingley, Cambridge*

17–21 July
1486 Bookbinding £AFD
Urchfont Manor College *Devizes*
ARCA

17–23 July
1487 Macnaghten String
 Quartet summer
 school £250/290
Benslow Music Trust *Hitchin*
ARCA

18–21 July
1488 Forensic psychology £AFD
1489 Golf – intermediate £AFD
Knuston Hall *Irchester*
ARCA

18–21 July
1490 An introduction to garden
 design £AFD
West Dean College *Chichester*
ARCA

19–22 July
1491 Croquet – players £184
HF Holidays *Bourton-on-the-Water*

20–22 July
1492 Literature: Victorian
 encounters – publishers,
 editors and readers £80
Birkbeck College Univ London *London*

21–23 July
1493 Yoga £90
Alston Hall College *Preston*
ARCA

21–23 July
1494 Folk dancing £110
1495 Creative plaster casting
 and gilding £110
Burton Manor College *Neston, Cheshire*
ARCA

21–23 July
1496 A weekend of walking
 and natural history £89/114
1497 Rural rides £89/114
Field Studies Council *Juniper Hall Centre, Dorking, Surrey*

21–23 July
1498 Yellow composites £90/120
1499 The otter £85/115
Field Studies Council *Preston Montford, Shropshire*

21–23 July
1500 Sacred clowning £AFD
Hawkwood College *Stroud, Glos*
ARCA

21–23 July
1501 Bell ringing £AFD
Horncastle College *Horncastle*
ARCA

21–23 July
1502 Period style at Jackdaws
 (for observers only). The
 orchestra of the Age of
 Enlightenment £105*
Jackdaws Educational Trust *Frome, Somerset*
*food included. B & B extra

21–23 July
1503 Golf – beginners £107
1504 Ancient America £107
1505 Impressionism £107
Knuston Hall *Irchester*
ARCA

QUALITY STUDY BREAKS AT PLACES OF CHARACTER AND HISTORIC INTEREST

ARCA is a well-established association of Residential Colleges for Adult Education. It provides a wide range of quality short-stay courses for the general public. Some colleges are run by local authorities; others by charitable trusts or similar organisations. All share a professional approach to education in a residential setting and are wholeheartedly committed to the principle of "life-long learning"; learning for personal satisfaction and enjoyment.

It is this liberal approach to learning that is at the heart of ARCA. You do not need academic qualifications to enrol; all you need do is complete a booking form and return it with your fee. Telephone bookings and credit card payments are accepted by many colleges.

Attending an ARCA college can be a simple pleasure or an event, which looking back, you may see as a turning point in your life. A short-stay course can lead on to a formal course of study and to a recognised qualification.

Each college publishes its own programme of courses and will be glad to send you a copy.

Members of the Adult Residential Colleges Association are listed on the following pages with their postal and e-mail addresses, and telephone numbers.

•

A World of Adult Learning is at your fingertips

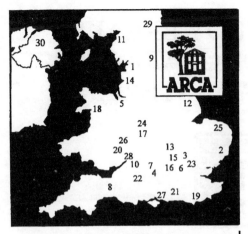

THE ARCA COLLEGES

1
Alston Hall College, LONGRIDGE,
Preston, Lancs PR3 3BP
Tel: 01772 784 661 Fax: 01772 785 835
e-mail: enquiries@alstonhall.u-net.com

2
Belstead House, Belstead, IPSWICH,
Suffolk IP8 3NA
Tel: 01473 686 321 Fax: 01473 686 664
e-mail: belsteadhouse@talk21.com

3
Benslow Music Trust, Little Benslow Hills,
Ibberson Way, HITCHIN, Herts SG4 9RB
Tel: 01462 459 446 Fax:01462 440 171
e-mail: BmusicT@aol.com

4
Braziers, Braziers Park, IPSDEN, Wallingford,
Oxon OX10 6AN Tel & Fax: 01491 682 402

5
Burton Manor College, BURTON,
South Wirral, Cheshire L64 5SJ
Tel: 0151 336 5172/3 Fax 0151 336 6586
e-mail: enquiries@burtonmanor.com

6
Debden House, Debden Green, LOUGHTON,
Essex IG10 2PA
Tel: 0181 508 3008 Fax: 0181 508 0284

7
Denman College, MARCHAM, Abingdon,
Oxon OX13 6NW
Tel: 01865 391 991 Fax: 01865 391 966

8
Dillington House, ILMINSTER, Somerset
TA19 9DT
Tel: 01460 52427 Fax: 01460 52433
e-mail: dillington@somerset.gov.uk

9
Grantley Hall, RIPON, North Yorkshire
HG4 3ET
Tel: 01765 620259/441 Fax: 01765 620441

10
Hawkwood College, Painswick Old Road,
STROUD, Gloucestershire GL6 7QW
Tel: 01453 759 034 Fax: 01453 764 607
e-mail: hawkwood@compuserve.com

11
Higham Hall, BASSENTHWAITE LAKE
Cockermouth, Cumbria CA13 9SH
Tel: 01768 776 276 Fax: 01768 776 013
e-mail: higham.hall@dial.pipex.com

12
Horncastle College; Mareham Road,
HORNCASTLE, Lincs, LN9 6BW
Tel: 01507 522 449 Fax: 01507 524 382
e-mail:
horncastle.college@lincolnshire.gov.uk

13
Knuston Hall, IRCHESTER,
Wellingborough, Northants NN29 7EW
Tel: 01933 312 104 Fax: 01933 357 590
e-mail: enquiries@knustonhall.org.uk

14
Lancashire College, Southport Road,
CHORLEY, Lancashire PR7 1NB
Tel: 01257 276 719 Fax: 01257 241 370
e-mail: insight@lancscollege.u-net.com

15
Maryland College, Leighton Street,
WOBURN, Beds MK17 9JD
Tel: 01525 292 901 Fax: 01525 290 051

16
Missenden Abbey, GREAT MISSENDEN
Bucks HP16 0BD
Tel: 01494 890 298 Fax: 01494 863 697
e-mail:
enquiries@missendenabbey.ac.uk

17
Pendrell Hall, CODSALL WOOD,
Wolverhampton, Staffs WV8 1QP
Tel: 01902 434 112 Fax: 01902 434 113
e-mail:
pendrell.college@staffordshire.gov.uk

18
Plas Tan y Bwlch; Snowdonia National Park Study Centre, MAENTWROG, Blaenau Ffestiniog, Gwynedd LL41 3YU
Tel: 01766 590 324 Fax: 01766 590 274
e-mail: plastanybwlch@compuserve.com

19
Pyke House, Upper Lake, BATTLE, East Sussex TN33 0AN
Tel: 01424 772 495 Fax: 01424 775 041
E-mail: hcatpykehouse@btinternet.com

20
The Hill Residential Centre, Pen-y-Pound, ABERGAVENNY, Gwent NP7 7RP
Tel: 01495 333 777 Fax: 01495 333 778
e-mail: hill@gwent-tertiary.ac.uk

21
The Old Rectory Adult Education College, FITTLEWORTH, Pulborough, W.Sussex RH20 1HU
Tel & Fax: 01798 865 306
e-mail: oldrectory@mistral.co.uk

22
Urchfont Manor, URCHFONT, Devizes, Wiltshire SN10 4RG
Tel: 01380 840 495 Fax 01380 840 005
e-mail: urchfont@wccyouth.org.uk

23
Wansfell College, Piercing Hill, THEYDON BOIS, Epping, Essex CM16 7LF
Tel: 01992 813 027 Fax:01992 814 761
e-mail: enquiries@wansfell.demon.co.uk

24
Wedgwood Memorial College, Station Road BARLASTON, Stoke-on-Trent, Staffs ST12 9DG
Tel: 01782 372 105 Fax: 01782 372 393
e-mail: wedgwood.college@staffordshire.gov.uk

25
Wensum Lodge, King Street, NORWICH, Norfolk NR1 1QW
Tel: 01603 666 021 Fax: 01603 765 633

26
Weobley Art Centre, The Old Corner House, Broad Street, WEOBLEY, Herefordshire HR4 8SA
Tel & Fax: 01544 318 548
e-mail:enquiries@weobley.demon.co.uk

27
West Dean College, WEST DEAN, Chichester, Sussex PO18 0QZ
Tel: 01243 811 301 Fax: 01243 811 343
e-mail: westdean@pavilion.co.uk

28
Wye Valley Arts Centre, Mork, St. Briavels, LYDNEY, Gloucestershire GL15 6QH
Tel: 01594 530 214 Fax: 01594 530 321
e-mail: wyeart@mcmail.com

29
Otterburn Hall, OTTERBURN Northumberland NE19 1HE
Tel: 01830 520 663 Fax: 01830 520491
e-mail: otterburn.hall@cwcom.net

30
The Rural College, Derrynoid, DRAPERSTOWN County DERRY BT45 7DW
Tel: 01648 29100 Fax: 01648 27777
e-mail: ruralcol@iol.ie

ADULT RESIDENTIAL COLLEGES ASSOCIATION

Secretary: Derek Barbanell,
PO Box 31, Washbrook, Ipswich IP8 3HP

Visit the
ARCA Website *at*
http://www.aredu.org.uk

THE ARCA SYMBOL IS YOUR SIGN OF QUALITY

ARCA colleges share an atmosphere unlike that of other educational institutions. Many are historic houses set in beautiful countryside, far from the pressures and distractions of everyday life; others may be Victorian or Edwardian family homes. However stately or modest their location, ARCA colleges proudly maintain a high standard in hospitality and tuition which is regularly monitored by the association.

Regular ARCA monitoring is your guarantee of quality in what is probably the best residential adult education in the country.

Fees vary from college to college. The comfortable accommodation may be simple or grandly en-suite. Staff are supportive and always ready to help. Most dietary needs can be supplied and many colleges offer facilities for people with disabilities.

Attending a short-stay residential course is a wonderful way of meeting new people. Through repeat visits strong friendships can form and regular learning breaks at ARCA colleges can easily become a way of life!

Adult Residential Colleges Association

21–23 July

1506	Willow crafts for beginners	£AFD
1507	Drawing with ink	£AFD
1508	ISAs and other investments	£AFD
1509	Build a Website	£AFD

Lancashire College *Chorley*
ARCA

21–23 July

| 1510 | Water colour painting | £89/115 |
| 1511 | The July countryside | £89/115 |

Maryland College *Woburn*
ARCA

21–23 July

| 1512 | China painting | £AFD |
| 1513 | Writing and marketing science fiction and fantasy | £AFD |

Pendrell Hall College *Staffs*
ARCA

21–23 July

| 1514 | Photography | £AFD |

Urchfont Manor College *Devizes*
ARCA

21–23 July

1515	Out and about from Wansfell	£104
1516	Practical painting	£89
1517	The hidden secrets of handwriting	£89

Wansfell College *Theydon Bois*
ARCA

21–23 July

| 1518 | Evolution of the English language | £80 |
| 1519 | Meditation to calm the mind | £80 |

Wedgwood Memorial College *Barlaston*
ARCA

21–24 July

| 1520 | Plants of saltmarshes and sand dunes | £117/150 |

Field Studies Council *Dale Fort Centre, Pembrokeshire*

21–24 July

1521	Villages and fine houses in Suffolk and Essex	£120/153
1522	Butterflies and moths of woodland, grassland and wetland	£120/153
1523	National Vegetation Classification: grassland and wetland habitats	£125/163
1524	Watercolour for near beginners	£120/153

Field Studies Council *Flatford Mill, Essex*

21–24 July

| 1525 | Mosses and liverworts of grassland and moorland | £125/160 |
| 1526 | Slugs and snails: critical identification of terrestrial molluscs | £113/145 |

Field Studies Council *Malham Tarn Field Centre, North Yorkshire*

21–25 July

| 1527 | Seascapes: exploring the Pembrokeshire coast | £148/190 |
| 1528 | Islands, birds and boating | £148/190 |

Field Studies Council *Dale Fort Centre, Pembrokeshire*

21–27 July

| 1529 | Calligraphy summer school | £295 |

Belstead House *Ipswich*
ARCA

21–28 July

| 1530 | Summer activity week 1 | £435 |

The Earnley Concourse *Chichester, Sussex*

Time to Learn

21–28 July
1531 Nature photography
 in high summer £243/313
1532 Working with a flora £238/305
Field Studies Council *Juniper Hall Centre, Dorking, Surrey*

21–28 July
1533 Archaeology of the
 limestone dales £230/295
1534 Introduction to
 fly fishing £253/325
Field Studies Council *Malham Tarn Field Centre, North Yorkshire*

21–28 July
1535 The geology and scenery
 of the borderland £185/290
Field Studies Council *Preston Montford, Shropshire*

21–28 July
1536 Environment for fun:
 a nature discovery
 week for families £AFD
Field Studies Council *Rhyd-y-creuau Centre, Snowdonia*

21–28 July
1537 Alberni masterclass £AFD
Univ Cambridge *Madingley, Cambridge*

22–23 July
1538 Mosaics £AFD
1539 Sculpture £AFD
1540 Photography £AFD
1541 Wood carving £AFD
Acorn Activities *Herefordshire*
1542 Stained glass £AFD
Acorn Activities *Shropshire*

22–25 July
1543 The theatre at Pitlochry £199
HF Holidays *Pitlochry*

22–26 July
1544 Harrogate international:
 music festival £314
HF Holidays *Malhamdale*

22–28 July
1545 Victorian Scotland £180
1546 Our global environment £165
Univ Edinburgh *Edinburgh*

22–28 July
1547 Watercolour still life £AFD
1548 Drawing and painting
 landscape £AFD
1549 Experimental stitched
 textiles £AFD
1550 Enamelling, art and craft £AFD
1551 Blacksmithing and design £AFD
1552 Sculptural ceramics and
 vessel £AFD
**West Dean College *Chichester*
ARCA**

22–29 July
1553 Heritage Lancashire £365
**Alston Hall College *Preston*
ARCA**

22–29 July
1554 Westonbirt summer
 school* £365
Birkbeck College Univ London *Nr Tetbury, Glos*
various subjects – see advertisement

22–29 July
1555 Silver light and reflections:
 drawing and painting
 in the Lake District £225/290
1556 Grasses, sedges
 and rushes £240/305
Field Studies Council *Blencathra, Lake District*

22–29 July
1557 Painting – soft pastels
 indoors £449
HF Holidays *Abingworth*

July — Time to Learn

1558	Flat green bowls – improvers	£404

HF Holidays *Bourton-on-the-Water*

1559	Landscape painting	£394

HF Holidays *Conwy*

1560	Landscape painting	£439

HF Holidays *Haytor, Devon*

1561	Landscape painting	£449

HF Holidays *Malhamdale*

22–29 July

1562	Patchwork	£AFD

Higham Hall *Cockermouth* **ARCA**

22–29 July

1563	Nineteenth century pioneers of geology	£420
1564	Hadrian's Wall: the ultimate frontier	£460

Summer Academy *Univ Durham*

1565	East Anglian market towns	£460
1566	Fire, plague and rebellion: medieval and Tudor Norwich	£460
1567	Creative writing	£460

Summer Academy *Univ East Anglia Norwich*

1568	The country house in the south west	£460
1569	From bathing machines to buckets and spades: the rise of the Devon seaside resorts	£460
1570	The green man	£460

Summer Academy *Univ Exeter*

1571	Hot summers and mild winters: the challenge of climatic change	£460
1572	Geology, landscape and wildlife	£460

Summer Academy *Univ Kent, Canterbury*

1573	Exploring ancient churches and their symbolism	£460
1574	Drawing and painting summer flowers in detail	£460
1575	Designing your garden	£460

Summer Academy *Univ Sheffield*

1576	Exploring Scotland's historic towns	£490

Summer Academy *Univ Stirling*

22–29 July

1577	Origins of human civilisation	£AFD
1578	The plantsman's garden	£AFD
1579	The demon drink: the social history of the English public house	£AFD
1580	Sails and paddles: the industrial archaeology of milling in the East Midlands	£AFD
1581	Country houses	£AFD
1582	Writing is fun	£AFD
1583	The Plantagenets and their architecture	£AFD
1584	Musical form explained	£AFD
1585	Classic horror – Dracula *et al*	£AFD
1586	Domesday – England at the last millennium	£AFD
1587	Creative applications of computing	£AFD
1588	The Millennium – an introduction to C20th art	£AFD
1589	Mosaic making	£AFD
1590	Landscape for the new millennium	£AFD
1591	Summer read	£AFD

Univ Nottingham *Nottingham*

22–31 July

1592	The Outer Hebrides: from Butt of Lewis to Sound of Harris	£1100

Field Studies Council Overseas *Outer Hebrides, Scotland*

23–27 July

1593	Pottery with other activities	£AFD

Acorn Activities *Herefordshire*

23–28 July

1594	Landscape painting	£AFD

Acorn Activities *Herefordshire*

23–28 July

1595	Chinese brush painting	£223
1596	Couture speed tailoring	£AFD

Alston Hall College *Preston* **ARCA**

23–28 July
1597 Impressionism £AFD
Knuston Hall *Irchester*
ARCA

23–29 July
1598 Romans in the north £AFD
Higham Hall *Cockermouth*
ARCA

23–29 July
1599 Painting the castles of
Herefordshire £439
Watercolour Weeks at Weobley
Weobley, Hereford

23 July–5 August
1600 Lampeter summer workshop
in Greek and Latin £240*
Univ Wales *Lampeter*
*price per week. Tuition only or full board

24–26 July
1601 Bridge £111
Burton Manor College *Neston, Cheshire*
ARCA

24–26 July
1602 This year's Proms £89
Wansfell College *Theydon Bois*
ARCA

24–27 July
1603 Morris to Makepeace:
a great craft legacy £146/185
Maryland College *Woburn*
ARCA

24–27 July
1604 Aspects of William Morris £110
Wedgwood Memorial College
Barlaston
ARCA

24–28 July
1605 Summer school in health
studies £224
Burton Manor College *Neston, Cheshire*
ARCA

24–28 July
1606 Creative calligraphy £153/196
1607 Drawing and painting
wildlife £153/196
Field Studies Council *Flatford Mill, Essex*

24–28 July
1608 The countryside in
summer: a family wildlife
discovery week £AFD
Field Studies Council *Juniper Hall Centre, Dorking, Surrey*

24–28 July
1609 Woodland mosses
and liverworts £144/185
1610 Flowers of the
limestone £144/185
Field Studies Council *Malham Tarn Field Centre, North Yorkshire*

24–28 July
1611 Furniture restoration/light
upholstery £AFD
1612 Life painting £AFD
Horncastle College *Horncastle*
ARCA

24–28 July
1613 Practical
woodcarving £156/220
Maryland College *Woburn*
ARCA

24–28 July
1614 Chinese brush painting £AFD
1615 Beadwork summer school £AFD
Pendrell Hall College *Staffs*
ARCA

acorn*activities*

For Britain's *best* Learning Breaks

All-year activity & special interest holidays nationwide. Holidays for singles, couples, families and groups. Corporate Entertainment and Gift Vouchers available. Hotels, Guest Houses, Farmhouse accommodation available.

IT'S NEVER TOO LATE TO LEARN OR IMPROVE YOUR SKILL

OVER 50 ARTS & CRAFTS	GARDEN DESIGN
PAINTING & DRAWING	WALKING & CYCLING
COUNTRY SPORTS	BALL SPORTS
AIR SPORTS	WATER SPORTS
MOTOR SPORTS	SPECIALIST PURSUITS

FOR YOUR FREE BROCHURE WITH OVER 100 ACTIVITIES CALL NOW ON

01432 830083

acorn*activities*

PO BOX 120, HEREFORD HR4 8YB
TEL: 01432 830083 - FAX 01432 830110
www.acornactivities.co.uk
info@acornactivities.co.uk

24–28 July
1616 Approaches to literature £AFD
Urchfont Manor College *Devizes*
ARCA

24–28 July
1617 Bookbinding summer
school £184
1618 Design your own garden £197
Wansfell College *Theydon Bois*
ARCA

24–29 July
1619 Literature summer school £AFD
Burton Manor College *Neston, Cheshire*
ARCA

24–29 July
1620 From stone circles to
early churches £160/200
Field Studies Council *Blencathra, Lake District*

25–26 July
1621 All gold bridal bouquets
(sugar or cold porcelain) £AFD
Pendrell Hall College *Staffs*
ARCA

25–29 July
1622 Benslow harp summer
school £220
1623 International flute
summer school £220/260
Benslow Music Trust *Hitchin*
ARCA

25–29 July
1624 The theatre at Pitlochry £259
HF Holidays *Pitlochry*

26–29 July
1625 Celtic inspirations –
painted and stitched
textiles £AFD
Dillington House *Ilminster*
ARCA

26–30 July
1626 Bugs, beasts and birds £AFD
Field Studies Council *Dale Fort Centre, Pembrokeshire*

26–30 July
1627 Family wildlife discovery £AFD
Field Studies Council *Orielton Centre, Pembrokeshire*

26–30 July
1628 Creation's stories with
words and colour £256/324
Hawkwood College *Stroud, Glos*
ARCA

26–30 July
1629 Unlocking the voice £105*
Jackdaws Educational Trust *Frome, Somerset*
*food included. B & B extra

26 July–2 August
1630 Woodland biodiversity
and management £233/290
1631 Family discovery week £AFD
1632 Out and about in west
Somerset £233/290
Field Studies Council *Nettlecombe Court Centre, Exmoor*

26 July–2 August
1633 Botanical illustration £218/280
Field Studies Council *Orielton Centre, Pembrokeshire*

27–28 July
1634 Strawberry fairy (sugar
or cold porcelain) £AFD
Pendrell Hall College *Staffs*
ARCA

27 July–4 August
1635 Marquetry summer
school £295
Belstead House *Ipswich*
ARCA

July — Time to Learn

28–30 July
1636 Sacred Gaia £80
1637 The new century of clowning £75
Ammerdown Centre *Radstock, Bath*

28–30 July
1638 Reiki second degree £305
1639 Chair caning for beginners £135
1640 Enamelling for everyone £110
Burton Manor College *Neston, Cheshire*
ARCA

28–30 July
1641 Improve your drawing skills £97/124
Field Studies Council *Juniper Hall Centre, Dorking, Surrey*

28–30 July
1642 Outdoor creativity for the young adventurer £AFD
1643 Discover the Dales in a weekend £86/110
Field Studies Council *Malham Tarn Field Centre, North Yorkshire*

28–30 July
1644 An inordinate fondness for beetles £90/120
1645 Ferns £85/115
Field Studies Council *Preston Montford, Shropshire*

28–30 July
1646 Decorative, embroidered boxes £107
1647 Needle lace – classic and contemporary £107
1648 Bucks point lace £107
1649 Bedfordshire lace £107
Knuston Hall *Irchester*
ARCA

28–30 July
1650 China painting for beginners £AFD
1651 Managing the quality business £AFD
1652 Change a room – first steps £AFD
Lancashire College *Chorley*
ARCA

28–30 July
1653 J.S. Bach £89/115
1654 Italian language – intermediate level £89/115
Maryland College *Woburn*
ARCA

28–30 July
1655 A heritage of Scottish song and verse £80/129
1656 Engineers of the human soul £80/129
1657 Greeks and Romans in the Holy Land £80/129
1658 Abbeys and priories in medieval England £80/129
Univ Cambridge *Madingley, Cambridge*

28–30 July
1659 Wine tasting weekend £AFD
1660 Creative plasterwork £AFD
Urchfont Manor College *Devizes*
ARCA

28–30 July
1661 Chamber music – wind and string ensembles £70/105
Wensum Lodge *Norwich*
ARCA

28–31 July
1662 Pastel painting for absolute beginners £120/153
1663 Suffolk's summer gardens £126/160
Field Studies Council *Flatford Mill, Essex*

28–31 July

1664 Water plants £145/190

Field Studies Council *Preston Montford, Shropshire*

28 July–2 August

1665 Birds of Anglesey £111

Burton Manor College *Neston, Cheshire*
ARCA

28 July–4 August

1666 Calligraphy summer school £220

1667 Woodcarving for all £220

Burton Manor College *Neston, Cheshire*
ARCA

28 July–4 August

1668 Summer school for singers £408

1669 Painting and sketching £408

1670 Drawing and painting for beginners £408

1671 Photographing nature £450

The Earnley Concourse *Chichester, Sussex*

28 July–4 August

1672 Improve your photography: the seeing eye £242/310

Field Studies Council *Flatford Mill, Essex*

28 July–4 August

1673 Mosses and liverworts £200/305

Field Studies Council *Preston Montford, Shropshire*

28 July–4 August

1674 Landscape painting in Snowdonia £203/280

1675 Wild flowers of Snowdonia and the north Wales coast £203/280

1676 Conservation gardening: wildlife havens and organic gardens £203/280

Field Studies Council *Rhyd-y-creuau Centre, Snowdonia*

28 July–4 August

1677 Paper, scissors, stone: a creative course for all the family £AFD

1678 Introduction to lichens £208/270

1679 Natural history photography £212/275

Field Studies Council *Slapton Ley Centre, Devon*

29 July–2 August

1680 Sussex on a bike £239

HF Holidays *Abingworth*

29 July–4 August

1681 Modern Scotland £180

Univ Edinburgh *Edinburgh*

29 July–4 August

1682 Waterways summer school £290

Wedgwood Memorial College *Barlaston*
ARCA

29 July–4 August

- 1683 Mosaics – texture, tone and colour — £AFD
- 1684 Silk screenprinting and beyond — £AFD
- 1685 Drawing from the model — £AFD
- 1686 Machine embroidery – wall mounted textiles — £AFD
- 1687 Stone carving — £AFD
- 1688 Sea themes – any media — £AFD
- 1689 Enamelling techniques in jewellery — £AFD
- 1690 Handbuilding ceramics — £AFD

**West Dean College *Chichester*
ARCA**

29 July–5 August

- 1691 Chamber music summer school — £320

**Alston Hall College *Preston*
ARCA**

29 July–5 August

- 1692 Westonbirt summer school* — £365

Birkbeck College Univ London *Nr Tetbury, Glos*
various subjects – see advertisement

29 July–5 August

- 1693 Taste of Pembrokeshire — £218/280
- 1694 Geology and scenery of the Pembrokeshire coast — £218/280

Field Studies Council *Dale Fort Centre, Pembrokeshire*

29 July–5 August

- 1695 Photography tour — £494

HF Holidays *Abingworth*

- 1696 Bridge and walking — £414

HF Holidays *Bourton-on-the-Water*

- 1697 Gilbert and Sullivan — £429

HF Holidays *Dovedale*

- 1698 Landscape painting — £314

HF Holidays *Isle of Arran*

- 1699 Landscape painting — £419

HF Holidays *Pitlochry*

- 1700 Landscape painting — £439

HF Holidays *St Ives*

- 1701 Music making and walking — £389

HF Holidays *Selworthy*

29 July–5 August

- 1702 Jazz performance — £AFD

**Higham Hall *Cockermouth*
ARCA**

29 July–5 August

- 1703 The land of the prince bishops — £460
- 1704 Exploring the craft of poetry — £390

Summer Academy *Univ Durham*

- 1705 East Anglians of the first millennium — £460
- 1706 Great estates and houses of East Anglia — £460

Summer Academy *Univ East Anglia Norwich*

- 1707 Thomas Hardy's Wessex — £460
- 1708 West Country gardens — £460
- 1709 Alfred the Great and the Vikings in south west England — £460

Summer Academy *Univ Exeter*

- 1710 The gardens of Kent: history, designs and planting — £490
- 1711 Information at your fingertips: the wonders of the World Wide Web — £460

Summer Academy *Univ Kent, Canterbury*

- 1712 Writers and their heritage — £460
- 1713 The social history of food and eating — £460
- 1714 A silver odyssey — £460

Summer Academy *Univ Sheffield*

- 1715 Understanding Scotland's history — £490

Summer Academy *Univ Stirling*

29 July–7 August

- 1716 Manx magic: marine biology and natural history on the Isle of Man — £960

Field Studies Council Overseas *Isle of Man*

Edinburgh COLLEGE of ART
Summer School

Beginners
Painting • Drawing
Portrait • Printmaking
Watercolour • Masterclasses
Life Modelling • Bronze Casting
Calligraphy • Tapestry • Sculpture
Ceramics • Stained Glass • Jewellery
Stone Carving • Textile Design
Digital, Web & CAD Design
Animation • Photography
Children • Portfolio Prep.
Lectures • Visits
... and more

For Info &
Brochure:
The Centre for Continuing Studies
Tel: 0131 221 6111
Fax/24hr tel: 0131 221 6109
email: continuing.studies@eca.ac.uk
www.eca.ac.uk

JUNE • JULY • AUGUST

THE UNIVERSITY OF BIRMINGHAM
School of Continuing Studies

Study Breaks in Britain and Abroad

In 2000 these will include:

The Pre-Raphaelites in London

Birds and Plants on the Hebridean Island of Islay

Creative Writing: Exploring the Short Story

Modern Art in New York

Cracow: The Art Treasury of Poland

For further details please contact the Publicity Office on 0121 414 5607/7259

Come to Edinburgh this summer!

- exciting choice of courses
- international atmosphere
- university accommodation
- academic credit
- lively social programme
- a wonderful city!

Contact us now for your free brochure:

Ursula Michels, Centre for Continuing Education, University of Edinburgh, 11 Buccleuch Place, Edinburgh EH8 9LW tel: 0131 650 4400/662 0783(24 hrs) cce@ed.ac.uk http://www.cce.ed.ac.uk

history • literature • art • architecture • archaeology • gaelic • ecology • scottish studies • ecology • creative writing • drama • film studies • edinburgh festival arts • & much more

PROMOTING EXCELLENCE IN TEACHING & RESEARCH

July — Time to Learn — July

29 July–11 August
1717 Film studies £230
Univ Edinburgh *Edinburgh*

29 July–18 August
1718 Drama from page to stage £390
Univ Edinburgh *Edinburgh*

30 July–4 August
1719 Big band summer school £240/280
Benslow Music Trust *Hitchin*
ARCA

30 July–4 August
1720 The scenery and natural history of the southern Lakes £165/211
1721 Discovery and adventure £130/180
1722 Have a go at outdoor adventure activities £165/211
1723 Have a go at natural art £165/211
Field Studies Council *Castle Head Centre, Lake District*

30 July–4 August
1724 Dramatic Devon: exploring landscapes from Dartmoor to the coast £150/195
Field Studies Council *Slapton Ley Centre, Devon*

30 July–4 August
1725 Bedfordshire lace £AFD
1726 Bucks and Bedfordshire lace – beginners £AFD
1727 Withof and Duchesse lace £AFD
1728 Tambour, Limerick and Carrickmacross lace £AFD
Knuston Hall *Irchester*
ARCA

30 July–5 August
1729 Guitar summer school £AFD
Dillington House *Ilminster*
ARCA

30 July–5 August
1730 Watercolour week £439
Watercolour Weeks at Weobley
Weobley, Hereford

30 July–26 August
1731 Missenden summer school (one week courses available) £AFD
Missenden Abbey *Great Missenden*
ARCA

31 July–2 August
1732 Woodcarving £AFD
Horncastle College *Horncastle*
ARCA

31 July–3 August
1733 Watercolour painting – flowers £AFD
Lancashire College *Chorley*
ARCA

31 July–4 August
1734 Cycling and walking in Constable Country £153/196
Field Studies Council *Flatford Mill, Essex*

31 July–4 August
1735 Butterflies and moths £144/185
1736 Watercolour painting £144/185
Field Studies Council *Malham Tarn Field Centre, North Yorkshire*

31 July–4 August
1737 The wonders of nature £AFD
1738 Family sketching £AFD
Field Studies Council *Preston Montford, Shropshire*

31 July–4 August
1739 Practical oil painting £156/220
Maryland College *Woburn*
ARCA

31 July–4 August
1740 Social and economic history of country house £AFD
1741 The genius of Gilbert and Sullivan £AFD
Univ Cambridge *Madingley, Cambridge*

31 July–4 August
1742 Calligraphy summer school £AFD
Urchfont Manor College *Devizes*
ARCA

31 July–7 August
1743 Painting summer landscapes in watercolour £242/310
Field Studies Council *Flatford Mill, Essex*

August 2000

August
1744 Pottery and print making: basics and beginnings in Summer Wineland £AFD
Lindsey-Ward Print-Making and Ceramics *Holmfirth, West Yorkshire*

1–4 August
1745 Garden design £130
Ammerdown Centre *Radstock, Bath*

1–18 August
1746 Absolute beginners £AFD
1747 Life drawing £AFD
1748 Painting in the studio £AFD
1749 Painting out of doors £AFD
1750 Watercolour painting £AFD
1751 Printmaking £AFD
1752 Tapestry £AFD
1753 Textile design £AFD
1754 Artist masterclasses £AFD
1755 Sculpture for outdoors £AFD
1756 Photography – beginners and advanced £AFD
1757 Film/video/animation £AFD
1758 Desktop publishing £AFD
1759 Ceramics/glaze £AFD
1760 Papermaking £AFD
Edinburgh College of Art *Edinburgh*

1–31 August
1761 Russian – individual tuition* £AFD
1762 French – individual tuition* £AFD
1763 Beginners' Welsh – individual tuition* £AFD
Meirionnydd Languages *Trawsfynydd, Gwynedd*
£50 per day, subject to availability. Reduced fees for groups of 2/3 people

2–5 August
1764 Belly dancing £189
HF Holidays *Abingworth*

2–9 August
1765 Landscape drawing and painting £201/262
1766 Painting plants and flowers £201/262
1767 Birds and butterflies in high summer £225/286
Field Studies Council *Nettlecombe Court Centre, Exmoor*

2–16 August

1768 Landscape drawing and painting £385/500
Field Studies Council *Nettlecombe Court Centre, Exmoor*

3–6 August

1769 Stained glass workshop £184
Burton Manor College *Neston, Cheshire*
ARCA

4–6 August

1770 Rural surprises weekend: rural life £AFD
Acorn Activities *Herefordshire*

4–6 August

1771 String orchestra weekend £101/121
1772 Banjo weekend £101/121
Benslow Music Trust *Hitchin*
ARCA

4–6 August

1773 Hand painted furniture £110
1774 Arabic dancing £110
Burton Manor College *Neston, Cheshire*
ARCA

4–6 August

1775 A weekend on bats £101/129
Field Studies Council *Flatford Mill, Essex*

4–6 August

1776 Look out for mammals: an identification workshop £69/112
Field Studies Council *Dale Fort Centre, Pembrokeshire*

4–6 August

1777 The dance in piano music £105*
Jackdaws Educational Trust *Frome, Somerset*
*food included. B & B extra

4–6 August

1778 Bedfordshire lace £107
1779 Beaded purses £107
1780 Chinese brush painting £107
Knuston Hall *Irchester*
ARCA

4–6 August

1781 The alternative art course using contemporary art practices £AFD
1782 Introduction to complementary therapies £AFD
1783 Numerology – how to plan your future £AFD
1784 The Stock Market explained £AFD
1785 Windows Housekeeping £AFD
Lancashire College *Chorley*
ARCA

4–6 August

1786 Oil painting £89/115
1787 Mozart's final year £89/115
Maryland College *Woburn*
ARCA

4–6 August

1788 Finding your way in the countryside £AFD
1789 T'ai Chi Chuan £AFD
1790 Beautiful batik £AFD
1791 Simply watercolour £AFD
The Old Rectory *Fittleworth*
ARCA

4–6 August

1792 War by sea and on land £135
Univ Birmingham *Ludlow*

Time to Learn

4–6 August
1793 Behind the mask: a history of Greek theatre £80/129
Univ Cambridge *Madingley, Cambridge*

4–6 August
1794 Silk painting with the microwave £AFD
Urchfont Manor College *Devizes*
ARCA

4–6 August
1795 Birdwatching in Norfolk and Suffolk £70/105
Wensum Lodge *Norwich*
ARCA

4–7 August
1796 Drawing and painting for families £AFD
1797 Painting with Gouache: introducing the techniques £120/153
Field Studies Council *Flatford Mill, Essex*

4–7 August
1798 Art and artists of Devon £159
HF Holidays *Thurlestone Sands*

4–7 August
1799 Rearranging the landscape: landscape history £AFD
1800 The thought of Herachlus £AFD
Univ Cambridge *Madingley, Cambridge*

4–9 August
1801 Diving the Skomer Marine Reserve and Pembrokeshire islands £234/300
Field Studies Council *Dale Fort Centre, Pembrokeshire*

4–11 August
1802 Painting summer school £295
Belstead House *Ipswich*
ARCA

4–11 August
1803 Watercolour painting: country houses and gardens £408
1804 Landscape painting £408
1805 Discovering English gardens £463
The Earnley Concourse *Chichester, Sussex*

4–11 August
1806 Understanding weather £230/295
1807 Activity week for the young family £AFD
1808 Introduction to dry stone walling £245/315
1809 Discover the Dales £230/295
Field Studies Council *Malham Tarn Field Centre, North Yorkshire*

4–11 August
1810 Access to adventure: canoeing, climbing and mountain biking £103/180
1811 Snowdonia National Park exploration £203/280
1812 Down the River Conwy: a natural and historical journey £203/280
Field Studies Council *Rhyd-y-creuau Centre, Snowdonia*

4–11 August
1813 Simply wildflowers £212/275
1814 Beside the sea: a family naturalists experience £AFD
1815 Rural rambles: green lanes to village inns £227/295
1816 Around Slapton Ley: a beginners course in painting and drawing £208/270
1817 Creative writing £208/270
Field Studies Council *Slapton Ley Centre, Devon*

BURTON MANOR COLLEGE

BURTON, NESTON,
CHESHIRE CH64 5SJ.
Telephone 0151-336 5172
Fax 0151-336 6586

DAY, MIDWEEK AND WEEKEND COURSES

Painting, Drawing, Art Summer School, Calligraphy Summer School, Writing, Literature Summer School, Photography, Tiffany Lampshade Making, Stained Glass Workshop, Willow Weaving, Decoupage, Hand Painted Furniture, Enamelling, Making and Renovating Tiles, Embroidery, Textiles, Dvorak, Classical Guitar Workshop. Summer Feast of Popular Music, Singing, Flamenco Dancing, Arabic Dancing, Line Dancing, Folk Dancing, Circle Dancing, Health Studies Summer School, Reiki, 1&2, & A Reiki Retreat, Spinal Touch, Aromatherapy, Astrological Psychology, History, Geology, Bird Watching, Astronomy, Computers for beginners, Demystifying the Web, Creating a Web page, Bridge.

Also starting October 2000 part-time courses in:
ISPA/IFA Diploma in Aromatherapy
Ceramic Restoration Diploma
City & Guilds Embroidery
Feng Shui Certificate

Ring or write for brochure and details.
Burton Manor lies in the centre of Burton, one of the prettiest villages in Wirral. It is an impressive Manor House and it stands in thirty acres of private grounds with ornamental gardens, terraces and woodland with views across the Dee to the Welsh Hills. We offer exciting and interesting courses in comfortable, friendly surroundings. Our accommodation is in single or double rooms, some en suite, with central heating, wash hand basins, tea and coffee making facilities. Wheelchair access and facilities for people with disabilities.

Easily accessible by road: 5 miles from M56. B.R. Chester and Liverpool.

5–6 August

1818 Silversmithing — £AFD
1819 Watercolour for the terrified — £AFD
1820 Pottery — £AFD
Acorn Activities *Herefordshire*
1821 Photography — £AFD
Acorn Activities *Scotland*

5–9 August

1822 China painting — £190
**Alston Hall College *Preston*
ARCA**

5–9 August

1823 Habitats and their conservation — £148/190
1824 Digital photography: an introduction to cameras and techniques — £148/190
Field Studies Council *Dale Fort Centre, Pembrokeshire*

5–9 August

1825 Snowdonia challenge: discover, explore, conserve — £95
Field Studies Council *Rhyd-y-creuau Centre, Snowdonia*

5–11 August

1826 How the train changed Scotland — £240
1827 Reportage at the Edinburgh Fringe/Festival — £255
Univ Edinburgh *Edinburgh*

5–11 August

1828 Painting the Staffordshire Landscape — £255
1829 Creative Expression in Drawing and Painting — £255
**Wedgwood Memorial College
Barlaston
ARCA**

5–11 August

1830 Tapestry weaving — £AFD
1831 Creative blacksmithing — £AFD
1832 Pottery including Raku — £AFD
1833 Watercolour – light and atmosphere — £AFD
1834 Making jewellery using decorative surfaces — £AFD
**West Dean College *Chichester*
ARCA**

5–12 August

1835 Baltimore style appliqué quilts — £315
**Alston Hall College *Preston*
ARCA**

5–12 August

1836 Making a picture — £439
HF Holidays *Bourton-on-the-Water*
1837 Vivaldi and friends — £426
HF Holidays *Brecon*
1838 Family cycling and walking — £339
HF Holidays *Dovedale*
1839 Painting boats and harbours — £449
HF Holidays *Whitby*

5–12 August

1840 Medieval towns in Northumbria — £460
1841 Country houses in Durham and Northumberland — £460
Summer Academy *Univ Durham*
1842 East Anglian villages — £460
1843 Georgian taste and manners — £460
1844 Fried mice and violet pudding: exploring traditional and alternative medicine — £460
Summer Academy *Univ East Anglia, Norwich*
1845 Medieval pilgrimage — £460
1846 The history of the Cinque Ports — £460
Summer Academy *Univ Kent, Canterbury*
1847 From standing stones to Millennium Domes — £490
Summer Academy *Univ Stirling*

August   *Time to Learn*   **August**

1848 Wales new and old: language, culture and society £460

Summer Academy *Univ Wales, Swansea*

1849 The wild man of the woods £460

1850 Victorian times £460

Summer Academy *Univ York*

5–12 August

1851 Castles in Scotland £470

Univ Nottingham *Dundee*

6–11 August

1852 Scuba diving £AFD

Acorn Activities *Pembrokeshire*

6–11 August

1853 Painting £AFD

**Higham Hall *Cockermouth*
ARCA**

6–11 August

1854 Chinese brush painting £AFD

1855 Intensive Italian – intermediate and improvers £AFD

**Knuston Hall *Irchester*
ARCA**

6–12 August

1856 Bridge and walking £AFD

**Higham Hall *Cockermouth*
ARCA**

6–12 August

1857 Watercolour week £439

**Watercolour Weeks at Weobley
*Weobley, Hereford***

7–11 August

1858 Improve your pastel painting £153/196

1859 Painting in Constable Country: your own choice of media £153/196

1860 Surveying invertebrates in woodland, wetland and coastal habitats £153/196

1861 Family wildlife week £AFD

Field Studies Council *Flatford Mill, Essex*

7–11 August

1862 Horse riding £289

HF Holidays *Thurlestone Sands*

7–11 August

1863 Calligraphy £156/220

1864 Introduction to computers and word processing £156/220

**Maryland College *Woburn*
ARCA**

7–11 August

1865 Close-up-view: practical painting £AFD

1866 Field survey week £AFD

1867 Britain between the wars £AFD

Univ Cambridge *Madingley, Cambridge*

7–13 August

1868 Summer art school £342

**Burton Manor College *Neston, Cheshire*
ARCA**

7–25 August

1869 Piano workshop £465

Univ Edinburgh *Edinburgh*

9–12 August

1870 Landscape painting £192

HF Holidays *Sedbergh*

August — Time to Learn

9–13 August
1871 Living in comfort £210
Alston Hall College *Preston*
ARCA

9–16 August
1872 Natural history in
west Somerset £225/286
1873 Landscape drawing
and painting £201/262
Field Studies Council *Nettlecombe Court Centre, Exmoor*

11–13 August
1874 Renovating and
making tiles £110
Burton Manor College *Neston, Cheshire*
ARCA

11–13 August
1875 Docks and knotweeds £90/120
Field Studies Council *Preston Montford, Shropshire*

11–13 August
1876 Moths in a maritime
climate £104/135
Field Studies Council *Slapton Ley Centre, Devon*

11–13 August
1877 Oboe weekend £105*
Jackdaws Educational Trust *Frome, Somerset*
*food included. B & B extra

11–13 August
1878 Lacemaking £107
1879 Embroidery £107
1880 Clothes making £107
Knuston Hall *Irchester*
ARCA

11–13 August
1881 Computing for absolute
beginners £AFD
Lancashire College *Chorley*
ARCA

11–13 August
1882 Life and times of
Jesus £80/129
Univ Cambridge *Madingley, Cambridge*

11–13 August
1883 Exploring crop circles £AFD
Urchfont Manor College *Devizes*
ARCA

11–13 August
1884 Cabinet making – part 1 £AFD
1885 Small and vibrant still
life – waterbased media £AFD
1886 Microwave dyeing for
textured textiles £AFD
1887 Portraits in pastel £AFD
West Dean College *Chichester*
ARCA

11–14 August
1888 Exploring coasts and
seashores £120/153
1889 Painting in oils and
acrylics: rivers, coasts
and seascapes £120/153
1890 Improve your
watercolours £120/153
Field Studies Council *Flatford Mill, Essex*

11–14 August
1891 Seeing stars £92/120
1892 Dandelions, daisies
and thistles £127/165
Field Studies Council *Slapton Ley Centre, Devon*

11–14 August
1893 Devon on a bike £139
HF Holidays *Thurlestone Sands*

August — Time to Learn — August

11–15 August
1894 The healing elements of Pembrokeshire £148/190
Field Studies Council *Dale Fort Centre, Pembrokeshire*

11–18 August
1895 Country dance summer school £295
Belstead House *Ipswich* ARCA

11–18 August
1896 Summery activity week 2 £435
The Earnley Concourse *Chichester, Sussex*

11–18 August
1897 Botanical illustration for more experienced painters £242/310
Field Studies Council *Flatford Mill, Essex*

11–18 August
1898 Painting late summer flowers and fruits in watercolour £226/290
1899 Butterflies and moths in south-east England: their ecology and conservation £230/295
Field Studies Council *Juniper Hall Centre, Dorking, Surrey*

11–18 August
1900 Family activity week £AFD
1901 Introduction to the industrial archaeology of the Dales £230/295
1902 Landscape photography in the Dales £230/295
1903 Fens and bogs: the ecology of peatlands £230/295
Field Studies Council *Malham Tarn Field Centre, North Yorkshire*

11–18 August
1904 The Severn Way £165/270
1905 Using the National Vegetation Classification: swamps, fens, mires and aquatic communities £200/305
1906 Flower show, fireworks and fine gardens £200/305
Field Studies Council *Preston Montford, Shropshire*

11–18 August
1907 Family adventure week in Wales £AFD
Field Studies Council *Rhyd-y-creuau Centre, Snowdonia*

11–18 August
1908 Family naturalists £AFD
1909 Experiencing the landscape through painting and drawing £212/275
1910 Walking England's edge £212/275
Field Studies Council *Slapton Ley Centre, Devon*

11–18 August
1911 Spanish language school £AFD
Lancashire College *Chorley* ARCA

11–18 August
1912 Painting workshop for all £AFD
1913 Chinese brush painting £AFD
1914 Fabrics, threads and creative techniques £AFD
The Old Rectory *Fittleworth* ARCA

11–18 August
1915 Her infinite variety: a combination of painting and literature £AFD
Univ Cambridge *Madingley, Cambridge*

12–13 August
1916 Spinning £AFD
Acorn Activities *Brecon*

Abergavenny 'the Hill' Campus

The Hill is one of the largest residential colleges for adults in the country and is part of Gwent Tertiary College, the largest further education college in Wales. A country house in a wonderful setting on the fringes of the Brecon Beacons National Park, with accommodation for up to 80 people and emphasis on personal friendly service, The Hill is an ideal place for an enjoyable weekend or longer summer school course. The Hill provides a popular venue for mid-week meetings, seminars, management or business training, with the opportunity to unwind from intensive training in lovely surroundings with good food and bar facilities.

The Hill offers over 150 courses every year in subjects from History to Yoga, Bach to Computers, Internet to Bridge, plus our specialist Welsh, Welsh History and Welsh Culture courses. Our art studios, located in the former stable block, are used for an extensive range of garden, art and craft courses led by our team of experts.

The Hill has a programme of upgrading its rooms and facilities and recent changes include new computer rooms offering a popular range of courses on computing, software packages, the internet and small business skills.

Most of our accommodation is in comfortable, single-study bedrooms, including an increasing number with private facilities.

For further information and a copy of our current prospectus, please contact:

**Abergavenny 'the Hill' Campus, Pen-y-Pound,
Abergavenny, Gwent NP7 7RP
Telephone: 01495 333777, Fax: 01495 333778**

The College is situated in ten acres of landscaped private grounds in rural Staffordshire. Easy access from M6/M54. Wide range of weekend and mid-week courses held in a friendly relaxed atmosphere. Excellent food and licensed bar. Available for use as a venue for Conferences, Staff Training Courses, Seminars and Private Functions.

PENDRELL HALL

Codsall Wood, Staffs, WV8 1QP
Tel: 01902-434112
Fax: 01902-434113
E-mail:pendrell.college@staffordshire.gov.uk

SUMMER WINELAND
Basics and Beginnings

Pottery and print-making courses of two days or more, tailored to individual needs and dates.

Give yourself **TIME TO LEARN** the fundamentals of working with clay, making your own prints, or simply extending your existing skills, under expert, qualified tuition, in an early ninteenth century house, set in the Pennine Hills.

Work and develop at your own pace in a small group receiving individual teaching and personal attention. **Relax and enjoy!**
To obtain further information and details, write (enclosing SAE) or telephone:

John and Judith Ward
Lindsey-Ward Print-making and Ceramics
Hey Cottage, 64 Back Lane
Holmfith, West Yorks HD7 1HG
Tel: 01484 683428

1917 Drawing for the terrified £AFD
Acorn Activities *Herefordshire*

12–16 August
1918 Discovery, exploration and conservation for families £AFD
Field Studies Council *Rhyd-y-creuau Centre, Snowdonia*

12–16 August
1919 Cotswolds on a bike £234
HF Holidays *Bourton-on-the-Water*

12–18 August
1920 Film festival £175
1921 The Edinburgh Fringe £195
Univ Edinburgh *Edinburgh*

12–18 August
1922 Esperanto summer school £186
Wedgwood Memorial College *Barlaston*
ARCA

12–18 August
1923 Annual summer school in early music performance £AFD
West Dean College *Chichester*
ARCA

12–19 August
1924 Summer school of painting and drawing £305
Alston Hall College *Preston*
ARCA

12–19 August
1925 Drawing and painting £225/290
1926 Mosses and liverworts £230/295
Field Studies Council *Blencathra, Lake District*

12–19 August
1927 Landscape painting £399
1928 Photography tour £429
HF Holidays *Freshwater Bay*
1929 Music making and walking £434
HF Holidays *Malhamdale*
1930 Landscape painting £439
HF Holidays *Selworthy*

12–19 August
1931 Botanical illustration £AFD
1932 Walking £AFD
Higham Hall *Cockermouth*
ARCA

12–19 August
1933 Writing in wartime: drama, propaganda, realism, fiction and retrospect £460
1934 Kent houses and their families £490
Summer Academy *Univ Kent, Canterbury*
1935 Stirling: the hub of Scottish history £490
Summer Academy *Univ Stirling*
1936 Charles Rennie Mackintosh and the Glasgow style £490
1937 Great Scots who changed the world £490
Summer Academy *Univ Strathclyde, Glasgow*
1938 The medieval church – architecture and imagery £460
1939 Behind the scenes at the National Trust in Yorkshire £460
Summer Academy *Univ York*

13–17 August
1940 Pottery with other activities £AFD
Acorn Activities *Herefordshire*

13–18 August
1941 Landscape painting £AFD
Acorn Activities *Derbyshire Peak District*

August — Time to Learn — August

13–18 August
1942 Red rose rivers £230
**Alston Hall College *Preston*
ARCA**

13–18 August
1943 Lacemaking £AFD
1944 Embroidery £AFD
1945 Clothes making £AFD
**Knuston Hall *Irchester*
ARCA**

13–18 August
1946 Watercolour painting £AFD
1947 Sculptural ceramics £AFD
1948 Botanical illustration £AFD
1949 Fine furniture – traditional
 hand finishing £AFD
**West Dean College *Chichester*
ARCA**

13–19 August
1950 Identifying ferns £205/265
Field Studies Council *Blencathra, Lake District*

13–19 August
1951 Drawing and watercolour
 for the beginner £439
**Watercolour Weeks at Weobley
*Weobley, Hereford***

14–18 August
1952 Soul-making for women £150
1953 Medieval Celtic spirituality £160
Ammerdown Centre *Radstock, Bath*

14–18 August
1954 Write a successful novel £220
**Burton Manor College *Neston, Cheshire*
ARCA**

14–18 August
1955 Cycling and walking in
 Constable Country £153/196
1956 Painting in oils and
 acrylics: Suffolk skies
 and landscapes £153/196
1957 Family wildlife week £AFD
Field Studies Council *Flatford Mill, Essex*

14–18 August
1958 Butterflies and moths £180/230
Field Studies Council *Preston Montford, Shropshire*

14–18 August
1959 The mammals of
 Slapton Ley £130/170
1960 Butterflies and moths £125/160
Field Studies Council *Slapton Ley Centre, Devon*

14–18 August
1961 Know your angels £AFD
**Hawkwood College *Stroud, Glos*
ARCA**

14–18 August
1962 City of Rome £AFD
1963 The writer's craft £AFD
1964 Practical organ course £AFD
Univ Cambridge *Madingley, Cambridge*

14–18 August
1965 The European
 Renaissance £AFD
**Urchfont Manor College *Devizes*
ARCA**

14–20 August
1966 Benslow orchestra
 summer school £250/290
**Benslow Music Trust *Hitchin*
ARCA**

August   *Time to Learn*   **August**

14–20 August

1967 Machine knitting summer school £AFD

Urchfont Manor College *Devizes*
ARCA

16–18 August

1968 Golf – intermediate £AFD

Knuston Hall *Irchester*
ARCA

16–23 August

1969 Summer landscape in watercolour £201/262

1970 Shell life £225/286

Field Studies Council *Nettlecombe Court Centre, Exmoor*

18–20 August

1971 Elgar weekend: his life and music £AFD

Acorn Activities *Herefordshire*

18–20 August

1972 Discover the power of your natural voice £90

Alston Hall College *Preston*
ARCA

18–20 August

1973 Music 2000 £AFD

1974 Make a movie £110

Burton Manor College *Neston, Cheshire*
ARCA

18–20 August

1975 In search of bats £87/112

Field Studies Council *Castle Head Centre, Lake District*

18–20 August

1976 Cabbages, cresses and other crucifers £97/124

1977 Introducing ants £89/114

1978 Look out for mammals: an identification workshop £69/112

Field Studies Council *Juniper Hall Centre, Dorking, Surrey*

18–20 August

1979 Walking the Three Peaks £86/110

Field Studies Council *Malham Tarn Field Centre, North Yorkshire*

18–20 August

1980 Introduction to tree identification £85/115

1981 An introduction to freshwater invertebrates in still waters £90/120

1982 Painting and relaxation – choose your medium £85/115

Field Studies Council *Preston Montford, Shropshire*

18–20 August

1983 Bassoon weekend £105*

Jackdaws Educational Trust *Frome, Somerset*
food included. B & B extra

18–20 August

1984 Video camcorder £AFD

1985 Mah Jong for addicts £107

1986 An introduction to paper marbling £107

1987 Watercolour, beginners and beyond £107

Knuston Hall *Irchester*
ARCA

18–20 August

1988 Cultivating business excellence £AFD

Lancshire College *Chorley*
ARCA

18-20 August

1989 Alexander the Great £80/129
1990 Owls £80/129

Univ Cambridge *Madingley, Cambridge*

18-20 August

1991 Meditation to quieten the mind £AFD

Urchfont Manor College *Devizes*
ARCA

18-20 August

1992 Esperanto – 40th anniversary £76

Wedgwood Memorial College
Barlaston
ARCA

18-20 August

1993 Basketmaking – using flat paper cord £AFD
1994 Mosaic for exterior use £AFD
1995 A masterclass for singers £AFD

West Dean College *Chichester*
ARCA

18-21 August

1996 New directions in watercolour £120/153
1997 Painting flowers and trees in a Suffolk garden £124/157
1998 Creative writing in Constable Country £120/153
1999 Improve your painting: mastering the problems of foreground £120/153

Field Studies Council *Flatford Mill,*
Essex

18-21 August

2000 The hidden uses and meanings of plants £113/146

Field Studies Council *Rhyd-y-creuau*
Centre, Snowdonia

18-22 August

2001 Steaming through Snowdonia £194/238

Field Studies Council *Rhyd-y-creuau*
Centre, Snowdonia

18-25 August

2002 Rambling holiday £260
2003 Family holiday £AFD

Ammerdown Centre *Radstock, Bath*

18-25 August

2004 Painting summer school £295

Belstead House *Ipswich*
ARCA

18-25 August

2005 Landscape painting in watercolours £408
2006 Watercolour workshop £408
2007 Literary landscapes £463

The Earnley Concourse *Chichester,*
Sussex

18-25 August

2008 Landscape painting and drawing £226/290

Field Studies Council *Juniper Hall*
Centre, Dorking, Surrey

18-25 August

2009 Family nature week £AFD

Field Studies Council *Malham Tarn*
Field Centre, North Yorkshire

18-25 August

2010 Exploring Offa's Dyke £165/270
2011 Castles, gardens and tea shoppes £185/290

Field Studies Council *Preston*
Montford, Shropshire

What is happening at Lancaster this summer?

Special interest holiday courses & activities
23 July - 5 August 2000

Arts • Crafts • Writing • Computing • Walking • History & Culture
Study Skills • Exploring the Lake District • and much more

Adults and children welcome • Friendly atmosphere
Evening events • Residential or non residential
Close to Lakes and Dales

For details call **01524 592624** or visit our website
http://www.lancs.ac.uk.users.conted/

Department of Continuing Education, Lancaster University,
Lonsdale College, Lancaster LA1 1TH
Email Conted@lancaster.ac.uk

WEST DEAN COLLEGE

A LEADING ADULT RESIDENTIAL COLLEGE FOR CONTINUING EDUCATION IN THE ARTS AND THE CRAFTS

The College runs an extensive programme of weekend and week courses in the visual arts, contemporary and traditional crafts, photography, music and gardening for students of all levels. Courses take place in well-equipped workshops and studios, and tutors are also established practitioners. The historic house and landscaped gardens provide an inspirational setting. The College offers stimulating company, good accommodation and fine food.

CREATIVE ARTS SUMMER SCHOOL: 22-28 July, 29 July-August 4, 5-11 August
SUMMER SCHOOL IN EARLY MUSIC PERFORMANCE: 12-18 August

A full short course programme is available from:
WEST DEAN COLLEGE, (TL), WEST DEAN, CHICHESTER,
WEST SUSSEX PO18 OQZ T 01243 811301   F 01243 811343
E-mail: westdean@pavilion.co.uk   http://www.westdean.org.uk/

August — Time to Learn — August

18–25 August
2012 Natural history experience: Snowdonia and north Wales £AFD
Field Studies Council *Rhyd-y-creuau Centre, Snowdonia*

18–25 August
2013 Flowers in the landscape £AFD
2014 Summer walks on the wild side £AFD
2015 A week of eastern promise £AFD
The Old Rectory *Fittleworth* ARCA

18–27 August
2016 Silversmithing summer school £AFD
West Dean College *Chichester* ARCA

19–20 August
2017 Stained glass £AFD
Acorn Activities *Shropshire*
2018 Dry stone walling £AFD
Acorn Activities *Shropshire/Welsh Border*

19–22 August
2019 Bridge – improvers £159
HF Holidays *Pitlochry*

19–25 August
2020 Impressionist landscape £276
Alston Hall College *Preston* ARCA

19–25 August
2021 Reportage at the Edinburgh Fringe/Festival £255
2022 Music, theatre and dance at the Edinburgh Festival £240
2023 New writing in English: short story £130
Univ Edinburgh *Edinburgh*

19–26 August
2024 Evolution of the Lake District landscape £225/290
2025 Scenery and geology of the Lake District £230/295
2026 Wilder corners of Cumbria £230/295
Field Studies Council *Blencathra, Lake District*

19–26 August
2027 Gilbert and Sullivan £419
HF Holidays *Brecon*
2028 International folk dancing for all £349
HF Holidays *Conwy*
2029 Scottish dancing and walking – level 3 £389
HF Holidays *Derwentwater*
2030 Scottish country dancing – level 2 £349
HF Holidays *Freshwater Bay*
2031 Landscape painting £439
HF Holidays *Haytor, Devon*
2032 Music making for families £384
HF Holidays *Selworthy*

19–26 August
2033 Painting development £AFD
2034 Walks with a sketchbook £AFD
Higham Hall *Cockermouth* ARCA

19–26 August
2035 The Victorian novel £460
2036 The origins of Christianity in Britain – a Millennium perspective £460
Summer Academy *Univ Kent, Canterbury*
2037 The Victorian city: Manchester in perspective £490
2038 The condensed evolution of life on earth ... in one week £460
Summer Academy *UMIST (Manchester)*
2039 In search of Scottish history, literature and myth £490
Summer Academy *Univ Stirling*

| August | Time to Learn | August |

2040 Scottish historical homes and gardens £490
2041 Archaeology in west and central Scotland £490
Summer Academy Univ Strathclyde, Glasgow
2042 York: the first thousand years £460
2043 Castles and cottages of Yorkshire £460
Summer Academy Univ York

20–23 August
2044 Aspects of antiques £AFD
2045 Past life regression £AFD
2046 The tyranny of the Um-Cha-Cha £AFD
Dillington House Ilminster ARCA

20–23 August
2047 Woodturning £AFD
West Dean College Chichester ARCA

20–24 August
2048 Pottery with other activities £AFD
Acorn Activities Herefordshire

20–25 August
2049 Bobbin lace £223
2050 Summer school of calligraphy £223
Alston Hall College Preston ARCA

20–25 August
2051 Greenwood working £165/211
Field Studies Council Castle Head Centre, Lake District

20–25 August
2052 Exploring watercolour techniques £AFD
2053 Saxophone summer school £AFD
Knuston Hall Irchester ARCA

20–26 August
2054 Further pen and ink with watercolour £439
Watercolour Weeks at Weobley Weobley, Hereford

20–27 August
2055 Wind plus – summer school £280/320
Benslow Music Trust Hitchin ARCA

21–23 August
2056 Computers for beginners £198
Burton Manor College Neston, Cheshire ARCA

21–24 August
2057 Reiki retreat £AFD
Burton Manor College Neston, Cheshire ARCA

21–25 August
2058 Bead jewellery summer school £201
Belstead House Ipswich ARCA

21–25 August
2059 Painting plants: summer colours £153/196
2060 Family wildlife week £AFD
2061 Painting and drawing for families £AFD
2062 The pleasures of Plein Air painting £AFD
Field Studies Council Flatford Mill, Essex

21–25 August
2063 The countryside in late summer: a family wildlife discovery week £AFD
Field Studies Council Juniper Hall Centre, Dorking, Surrey

21-25 August
2064 Painting in the Dales £160/205
2065 Underground adventure £172/220
2066 Writing your own stories and poems £144/185
Field Studies Council *Malham Tarn Field Centre, North Yorkshire*

21-25 August
2067 Superstitions, myth and magic: an alternative look at British wildlife £148/192
Field Studies Council *Rhyd-y-creuau Centre, Snowdonia*

21-25 August
2068 Latin week £AFD
2069 French week £AFD
2070 Creative writing £AFD
2071 Botanical illustration £AFD
Univ Cambridge *Madingley, Cambridge*

21-25 August
2072 The world of Jane Austen £AFD
2073 Painting and sketching the Urchfont landscape £AFD
Urchfont Manor College *Devizes* ARCA

21-28 August
2074 Discovery and adventure – young leaders £180/250
2075 Discovery and adventure II £180/250
Field Studies Council *Castle Head Centre, Lake District*

22-26 August
2076 Bridge – improvers £209
HF Holidays *Pitlochry*

22-27 August
2077 Flute master class £AFD
West Dean College *Chichester* ARCA

23-30 August
2078 Exploring west Somerset £225/286
Field Studies Council *Nettlecombe Court Centre, Exmoor*

23-30 August
2079 A celebration of railway history £460
Summer Academy *Univ Durham*

25-27 August
2080 Music appreciation £90
Alston Hall College *Preston* ARCA

25-27 August
2081 Late summer walking weekend: exploring Suffolk's countryside £89/114
2082 Papermaking using natural and recycled materials £89/114
2083 Improve your watercolours £89/114
Field Studies Council *Flatford Mill, Essex*

25-27 August
2084 Identifying stream and river invertebrates £97/124
2085 Pastel weekend £97/124
Field Studies Council *Juniper Hall Centre, Dorking, Surrey*

25-27 August
2086 Look out for mammals: an identification workshop £69/112
Field Studies Council *Rhyd-y-creuau Centre, Snowdonia*

25-27 August
2087 Making mohair collectors bears £107
2088 Calligraphy £107
Knuston Hall *Irchester* ARCA

Time to Learn

HAWKWOOD COLLEGE

Short Residential Courses

Hawkwood College has been a centre for adult education since 1948. It is renowned for the beauty and peace of its setting in a Cotswold valley with view of the Severn Vale. It offers courses in music, science, arts and crafts, as well as an ideal venue for conferences and retreats.

For further information phone 01453 759034 or Fax 01453 764607 e-mail:hawkwood@compuserve.com

or write to

Hawkwood College
Painswick Old Rd
Stroud GL6 7QW

TIME TO LEARN

DON'T FORGET

When contacting the learning holiday organisers, please mention the fact that you found their details in TIME TO LEARN

WENSUM LODGE

Welcome to **Norfolk** and **Norwich** – an unspoilt corner of England, **Norfolk**, with its long attractive coastline, the famous Norfolk Broads, historic houses, medieval churches and open skies. **Norwich**, a beautiful and ancient Cathedral City, combining old world charm with a busy and commercial shopping centre, where music, and the arts, international cuisine and night-life, flourish.

Wensum Lodge, Norwich
Conversion of a former Victorian brewery site near to the city centre beide the River Wensum and includes a 12th-century historic house. Facilities include arts, crafts, theatre/studio and sports centre with squash courts and licensed bar. Accommodation is used for day and evening activity as well as a full and varied range of residential coures. Accommodates 38 people, mostly in twin-bedded rooms, often used as singles.

Postal Address: Wensum Lodge (CES), King Street, Norwich, NR1 1QW
Tel: 01603 666021/2 Fax: 01603 765633

ARCA

25–27 August
- 2089 How to make your own jewellery — £AFD
- 2090 Drawing birds and flowers in habitat with watercolours — £AFD
- 2091 Shakespeare for the terrified — £AFD
- 2092 Dowsing and divining – an introduction — £AFD
- 2093 Build a computer — £AFD

Lancashire College Chorley ARCA

25–28 August
- 2094 Forensic psychology weekend — £90

Alston Hall College Preston ARCA

25–28 August
- 2095 Vaughan-Williams: the symphonies — £232

The Earnley Concourse Chichester, Sussex

25–28 August
- 2096 Discovering the southern Lakes — £112/144

Field Studies Council Castle Head Centre, Lake District

25–28 August
- 2097 Bridge: improve your duplicate bridge — £190

Hawthorn Bridge Honiley, Nr Warwick

25–28 August
- 2098 Strings and things for violin and viola — £105*

Jackdaws Educational Trust Frome, Somerset
food included. B & B extra

25–29 August
- 2099 Clay modelling — £180

Alston Hall College Preston ARCA

25–29 August
- 2100 Steam in the south west — £125/160

Field Studies Council Slapton Ley Centre, Devon

25–30 August
- 2101 Geology — £AFD
- 2102 Advanced botanical illustration — £AFD
- 2103 Art and architecture of Imperial St Petersburg — £AFD
- 2104 Archaeology of the Nile — £AFD

Univ Cambridge Madingley, Cambridge

25 August–1 September
- 2105 Landscape painting — £408
- 2106 Life, landscape and portraiture — £408

The Earnley Concourse Chichester, Sussex

25 August–1 September
- 2107 Botanical illustration — £230/295
- 2108 Birds and bird migration — £234/300

Field Studies Council Juniper Hall Centre, Dorking, Surrey

26–29 August
- 2109 Painting boats and harbours — £171

HF Holidays Alnmouth

26–30 August
- 2110 The countryside in literature — £299

HF Holidays Bourton-on-the-Water
- 2111 Whist and walking — £209

HF Holidays Dovedale

26 August–1 September
- 2112 Music, theatre and dance at the Edinburgh Festival — £240
- 2113 New writing in English: poetry — £130

Univ Edinburgh Edinburgh

August — Time to Learn — August

26 August–2 September
2114 Lakeland life and tradition £230/295
2115 High peaks £230/295
2116 Water colour painting in the Lake District £225/290
2117 Walking from west to east £230/295
Field Studies Council *Blencathra, Lake District*

26 August–2 September
2118 Railways in the south east £499
HF Holidays *Abingworth*
2119 Opera and musicals £444
HF Holidays *Brecon*
2120 Get going, get fit £389
HF Holidays *Derwentwater*
2121 Croquet – beginners £359
HF Holidays *Freshwater Bay*
2122 Horse riding £599
HF Holidays *Haytor, Devon*
2123 Yoga and walking £369
HF Holidays *Isle of Arran*
2124 Drawing and walking £429
HF Holidays *St Ives*
2125 Bridge and sightseeing £419
HF Holidays *Whitby*

26 August–2 September
2126 Birds of Kent and the Channel shore £460
2127 English – the language of the world and the Millennium £420
Summer Academy *Univ Kent, Canterbury*
2128 Life on the seashores of Gower £460
2129 Reclaiming our ancient heritage: the prehistory of Gower, Britain and beyond £460
Summer Academy *Univ Wales, Swansea*
2130 The First World War and the commemoration of the fallen £460
2131 Life in a medieval city £460
Summer Academy *Univ York*

27–30 August
2132 Decorative fabric boxes £AFD
Knuston Hall *Irchester*
ARCA

27–30 August
2133 Small stone carvings £AFD
West Dean College *Chichester*
ARCA

27 August–1 September
2134 London Brass summer school £240/280
Benslow Music Trust *Hitchin*
ARCA

27 August–1 September
2135 Calligraphy £AFD
Knuston Hall *Irchester*
ARCA

27 August–1 September
2136 Silversmithing and jewellery £AFD
2137 Figure in the landscape £AFD
2138 Stained glass and glass painting £AFD
2139 Cane, willow and rush seating, basketry £AFD
West Dean College *Chichester*
ARCA

27 August–2 September
2140 Watercolour sketchbook week £439
Watercolour Weeks at Weobley *Weobley, Hereford*

28 August–1 September
2141 Painting £180
Alston Hall College *Preston*
ARCA

August — Time to Learn — August

28 August–1 September
2142 The countryside in late summer – a family wildlife discovery week £AFD
Field Studies Council *Juniper Hall Centre, Dorking, Surrey*

28 August–1 September
2143 Painting boats and harbours £214
HF Holidays *Thurlestone Sands*

28 August–1 September
2144 Geology £AFD
Univ Cambridge *Madingley, Cambridge*

28 August–1 September
2145 Lacemaking summer school £AFD
2146 The European Enlightenment £AFD
Urchfont Manor College *Devizes*
ARCA

28 August–2 September
2147 Kakkolistic summer school £265/350
Hawkwood College *Stroud, Glos*
ARCA

28 August–2 September
2148 The Great Scottish waterways £329
HF Holidays *Glen Coe*

28 August–3 September
2149 Millennium celebration for young people of Europe £150
Ammerdown Centre *Radstock, Bath*

29–30 August
2150 Miniature painting £58
Burton Manor College *Neston, Cheshire*
ARCA

29 August–1 September
2151 Egyptology £158
Burton Manor College *Neston, Cheshire*
ARCA

29 August–1 September
2152 Learn le Rock 'n' jive £199
HF Holidays *Alnmouth*

30 August–1 September
2153 Tomb-robbers, treasure hunters and archaeologists: the rediscovery of Ancient Egypt £90
Alston Hall College *Preston*
ARCA

30 August–1 September
2154 Still life £110
Burton Manor College *Neston, Cheshire*
ARCA

30 August–2 September
2155 Rocky shore invertebrates £117/150
2156 Exploring seashores: a family discovery holiday £AFD
Field Studies Council *Dale Fort Centre, Pembrokeshire*

30 August–2 September
2157 Composers of Gloucestershire £219
HF Holidays *Bourton-on-the-Water*
2158 Whist and walking £154
HF Holidays *Dovedale*

30 August–3 September
2159 Bat ecology £152/194
Field Studies Council *Orielton Centre, Pembrokeshire*

30 August–6 September
2160 Landscape painting around Nettlecombe Court £201/262
Field Studies Council *Nettlecombe Court Centre, Exmoor*

| August | *Time to Learn* | September |

30 August–6 September
2161 Exploring the Pembrokeshire Coast National Park £218/280
Field Studies Council *Orielton Centre, Pembrokeshire*

31 August–3 September
2162 Microscopy £117/147
Belstead House *Ipswich*
ARCA

September 2000

September
2163 Learn to swim
(5 day course) £AFD
2164 Learn to ride
(2 day course) £AFD
2165 Learn to ride
(5 day course) £AFD
Acorn Activities *England and Scotland*
2166 Furniture restoration £AFD
2167 Woodwork £AFD
2168 Woodturning £AFD
Acorn Activities *Herefordshire*
2169 Chair making £AFD
Acorn Activities *Yorkshire*

September
2170 Pottery and print making: basics and beginnings in Summer Wineland £AFD
Lindsey-Ward Print-Making and Ceramics *Holmfirth, West Yorkshire*

1–3 September
2171 Charles Rennie Mackintosh: his life and designs £AFD
Acorn Activities *Scotland*

1–3 September
2172 Drawing for the terrified I £90
2173 Native American Indians £90
2174 Chords and scales on guitar £90
Alston Hall College *Preston*
ARCA

1–3 September
2175 Machine embroidery £78/98
Belstead House *Ipswich*
ARCA

1–3 September
2176 Botanical painting £110
2177 Improvers' bridge £111
Burton Manor College *Neston, Cheshire*
ARCA

1–3 September
2178 Line dancing for all £158
2179 Music by Bach and family – for recorder players £158
2180 Using MS Word – level 2 £188
The Earnley Concourse *Chichester, Sussex*

1–3 September
2181 Introduction to papermaking £97/125
Field Studies Council *Malham Tarn Field Centre, North Yorkshire*

1–3 September
2182 Baroque chamber music £105*
Jackdaws Educational Trust *Frome, Somerset*
**food included. B & B extra*

THE
Widest Choice

Over 600 special interest and leisure short courses each year at FSC Centres in some of the finest locations in England and Wales.

From natural history to walking; art to adventure activities plus a programme of overseas study tours – FSC offers the widest choice.

To find out more and receive our free brochures contact:

- Field Studies Council (TTL), Montford Bridge Shrewsbury SY4 1HW. Telephone: 01743 850674 Fax: 01743 850178 • www.field-studies-council.org

ENVIRONMENTAL UNDERSTANDING FOR ALL

RESIDENTIAL CRASH COURSES
IN SNOWDONIA NATIONAL PARK

RUSSIAN, FRENCH, WELSH
and
ENGLISH AS A FOREIGN LANGUAGE

MEIRIONNYDD LANGUAGES

POSTAL TUITION
Available on a pay-as-you-learn basis. Beginners first three lessons with tape. Thereafter all lessons individually designed according to need and progress.

Residential prices [Inclusive tuition, accommodation board]
Individual . . . £300 week.
Small group [max 3 people] £200 week. Weekend £75

Daphne Percival, Bodyfuddau, Trawsfyndd, Gwynedd, LL41 4UW
Tel: (01766) 540 553 www: meirionnydd.force9.co.uk

September — Time to Learn

1–3 September
2183 Troy, Troy, try again: history of the Trojans £107
2184 Spanish literature £107
2185 Folk weekend £107
Knuston Hall *Irchester*
ARCA

1–3 September
2186 Caring for the carer. A weekend for unpaid carers £AFD
Lancashire College *Chorley*
ARCA

1–3 September
2187 Places of good company: Georgian towns £135
Univ Birmingham *Ludlow*

1–3 September
2188 The early history and archaeology of south Asia £80/129
2189 Euripides' Bacchae £80/129
2190 A weekend with Jung £80/129
Univ Cambridge *Madingley, Cambridge*

1–3 September
2191 Yorkshire mills and mill towns £175
Univ Nottingham *Bradford*
2192 The seaside holiday £100
2193 Myths of the sea: a literary exploration £100
Univ Nottingham *Gibraltar Point*
2194 The music of Robert Schumann £165
Univ Nottingham *Wadham College, Oxford*

1–3 September
2195 Millennium summer weekend £AFD
Urchfont Manor College *Devizes*
ARCA

1–3 September
2196 The Holy Land and the Old Testament £80
Wedgwood Memorial College *Barlaston*
ARCA

1–3 September
2197 Introduction to silversmithing £AFD
2198 Calligraphy £AFD
2199 Intensive life drawing £AFD
2200 Music and St Petersburg (lectures) £AFD
2201 Caring for furniture £AFD
West Dean College *Chichester*
ARCA

1–4 September
2202 Identifying centipedes, millipedes and woodlice £120/153
Field Studies Council *Flatford Mill, Essex*

1–8 September
2203 Watercolour painting: Sussex villages £408
2204 Painting and sketching: rural rides £408
2205 Wildlife rambles in west Sussex £448
The Earnley Concourse *Chichester, Sussex*

1–8 September
2206 Exploring the Settle–Carlisle railway £253/325
2207 Landscape painting in the Dales £230/295
Field Studies Council *Malham Tarn Field Centre, North Yorkshire*

1–8 September
2208 Autumn birds of Snowdonia and the north Wales coast £203/280
Field Studies Council *Rhyd-y-creuau Centre, Snowdonia*

September — Time to Learn — September

1–8 September
2209 Autumn embroidery school £AFD
2210 The best of British musicals £AFD
2211 Painting the Weald and wildlife of Sussex £AFD
The Old Rectory *Fittleworth*
ARCA

1–30 September
2212 Russian – individual tuition* £AFD
2213 French – individual tuition* £AFD
2214 Beginners' Welsh – individual tuition* £AFD
Meirionnydd Languages *Trawsfynydd, Gwynedd*
*£50 per day, subject to availability. Reduced fees for groups of 2/3 people

2–3 September
2215 Silversmithing £AFD
2216 Pottery £AFD
Acorn Activities *Herefordshire*
2217 Flower garden £AFD
Acorn Activities *Scotland*

2–6 September
2218 Croquet – players £269
HF Holidays *Abingworth*
2219 Painting trees £249
HF Holidays *Brecon*
2220 Scrabble® – experienced £234
HF Holidays *Malhamdale*

2–9 September
2221 Landscape painting £399
HF Holidays *Freshwater Bay*
2222 Birdwatching £474
HF Holidays *Haytor, Devon*

2–9 September
2223 Mountains and waterfalls £460
Summer Academy *Univ Wales, Swansea*

3–7 September
2224 Adventures with fabric – dyeing and painting £AFD
West Dean College *Chichester*
ARCA

3–8 September
2225 Identifying conifers £160/200
Field Studies Council *Blencathra, Lake District*

3–8 September
2226 Painting in Constable Country with oils, acrylics or gouache £184/235
Field Studies Council *Flatford Mill, Essex*

3–8 September
2227 Harbours and seascapes in watercolour £AFD
2228 Drawing and painting landscape £AFD
2229 Cabinet making – part 2 £AFD
West Dean College *Chichester*
ARCA

3–9 September
2230 Watercolour week £439
Watercolour Weeks at Weobley *Weobley, Hereford*

3–10 September
2231 Landscape photography £240/310
Field Studies Council *Blencathra, Lake District*

4–8 September
2232 Identifying spiders £153/196
Field Studies Council *Flatford Mill, Essex*

4–8 September
2233 Working towards sustainability £152/195
Field Studies Council *Malham Tarn Field Centre, North Yorkshire*

September — Time to Learn — September

4–8 September
2234 Calligraphy weekend £AFD
Urchfont Manor College *Devizes*
ARCA

4–8 September
2235 It's not what you do but the way that you do it. Drawing and painting £155
Wedgwood Memorial College *Barlaston*
ARCA

4–11 September
2236 West Country holiday £265
Ammerdown Centre *Radstock, Bath*

5–7 September
2237 Intermediate wind chamber music £AFD
Benslow Music Trust *Hitchin*
ARCA

5–8 September
2238 Exploring Cambridge architecture £120/193
Univ Cambridge *Madingley, Cambridge*

6–9 September
2239 Theatre in the south £249
HF Holidays *Abingworth*
2240 Singing for pleasure £154
HF Holidays *Alnmouth*
2241 Oil painting £189
HF Holidays *Brecon*

6–13 September
2242 Watercolour for beginners £218/280
Field Studies Council *Orielton Centre, Pembrokeshire*

7–10 September
2243 Microscopy £117/147
Belstead House *Ipswich*
ARCA

7–10 September
2244 Preparation for a career in opera £105*
Jackdaws Educational Trust *Frome, Somerset*
*food included. B & B extra

8–10 September
2245 Massage for women £90
2246 Hardanger embroidery £90
2247 Counselling level I £90
Alston Hall College *Preston*
ARCA

8–10 September
2248 Clarinet weekend £AFD
Benslow Music Trust *Hitchin*
ARCA

8–10 September
2249 Dvorak and his pupils £110
Burton Manor College *Neston, Cheshire*
ARCA

8–10 September
2250 Watercolour for near beginners £89/114
Field Studies Council *Flatford Mill, Essex*

8–10 September
2251 Autumn spiders £97/124
Field Studies Council *Juniper Hall Centre, Dorking, Surrey*

8–10 September
2252 Look out for mammals: an identification workshop £69/112
Field Studies Council *Malham Tarn Field Centre, North Yorkshire*

8–10 September
2253 Botany for gardeners £85/115
Field Studies Council *Preston Montford, Shropshire*

Alston Hall Residential College

Situated in the heart of the Ribble Valley, Alston Hall offers a rich programme of day, weekend & residential courses throughout the year

Courses in Art, Crafts, Natural & Local History, Music, Literature and Complementary Therapies are our particular strengths

Sample our renowned home cooking and enjoy a warm Lancashire welcome in this charming Victorian country house. Ensuite bedrooms, a licensed bar and minibus pickup service are available

Your Sign of Quality

For further details and a free brochure please contact:
Alston Hall College, Alston Lane, Longridge,
Preston PR3 3BP.   Tel: 01772 784661
e-mail: enquiries@alstonhall.u-net.com
and www.alstonhall.u-net.com

Knuston Hall

RESIDENTIAL COLLEGE FOR ADULT EDUCATION & CONFERENCE CENTRE

★ An elegant Manor House, set in magnificent countryside in central Northamptonshire.

★ Home cooked food and comfortable accommodation in en-suite bedrooms.

★ A wide range of weekend and week courses held in a friendly and relaxed atmosphere.

★ Available for use as a venue for conferences, staff training courses and seminars.

For current programme send s.a.e. to: Dept.T.
Knuston Hall, Irchester, Wellingborough, Northants NN29 7EU
Tel: 01933 312104 Fax: 01933 357596
E:mail - enquiries@knustonhall.org.uk
W.W.W. - http://www.knustonhall.org.uk

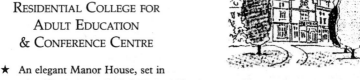

Northamptonshire

8–10 September
2254 Astronomy £AFD
Horncastle College *Horncastle*
ARCA

8–10 September
2255 Stumpwork £107
2256 Writing and illustrating £107
2257 Pastel painting £107
Knuston Hall *Irchester*
ARCA

8–10 September
2258 History alive –
 Egyptology £AFD
2259 Alexander Technique £AFD
2260 Separation and divorce –
 the facts £AFD
2261 Word processing – an
 introduction to MS WORD £AFD
Lancashire College *Chorley*
ARCA

8–10 September
2262 Bridge for experienced
 players £99/125
2263 Introduction to
 computers £99/125
Maryland College *Woburn*
ARCA

8–10 September
2264 Stained glass making £AFD
2265 Introduction to the
 Internet £AFD
2266 Watercolour workshop £AFD
2267 Wines of South Africa £AFD
The Old Rectory *Fittleworth*
ARCA

8–10 September
2268 Calligraphy £AFD
Pendrell Hall College *Staffs*
ARCA

8–10 September
2269 Chinese painting: a
 practical approach £135
Univ Birmingham *Ludlow*

8–10 September
2270 Elgar weekend £80/129
2271 The rebuilding of the
 Vatican and the
 Church of Rome:
 piety or propaganda? £80/129
2272 The green man £80/129
2273 Elgar, master of music £80/129
Univ Cambridge *Madingley, Cambridge*

8–10 September
2274 Churches in the
 Cotswolds £175
Univ Nottingham *Cheltenham*
2275 Medieval Durham £115
Univ Nottingham *Durham*

8–10 September
2276 Lacemaking £86
Wedgwood Memorial College
Barlaston
ARCA

8–10 September
2277 Watercolour –
 composition and three-
 dimensional effects £AFD
2278 Experimental batik
 on paper £AFD
2279 Creative watercolour £AFD
2280 The Bloomsbury Group
 painters (lectures and
 visits) £AFD
2281 Fine furniture making –
 part 1 £AFD
West Dean College *Chichester*
ARCA

8–11 September
2282 Hedgerow cookery £120/160
2283 Deer to dormice £120/160
Field Studies Council *Blencathra, Lake District*

8–11 September
2284 Recorder 2000 £145/190
Field Studies Council *Preston Montford, Shropshire*

8–11 September
2285 Japanese garden design £179
HF Holidays *Thurlestone Sands*

8–11 September
2286 Jewellery £AFD
West Dean College *Chichester*
ARCA

8–12 September
2287 Making ropes, cords
and tassels £AFD
West Dean College *Chichester*
ARCA

8–15 September
2288 Trees and woodlands
in the British
countryside £273/350
Field Studies Council *Flatford Mill, Essex*

8–15 September
2289 Landscape painting
in watercolours £180/285
Field Studies Council *Preston Montford, Shropshire*

9–10 September
2290 Stained glass £AFD
Acorn Activities *Shropshire*
2291 Flower garden £AFD
Acorn Activities *Worcestershire*

9–12 September
2292 The theatre at Pitlochry £194
HF Holidays *Pitlochry*

9–13 September
2293 The Brontës £289
HF Holidays *Malhamdale*

9–15 September
2294 Map and compass £336
HF Holidays *Conistonwater*

9–16 September
2295 Cotswold walks
of discovery £429
HF Holidays *Bourton-on-the-Water*
2296 Bridge and sightseeing £409
HF Holidays *Brecon*
2297 Landscape painting £409
HF Holidays *Derwentwater*
2298 Railways in the
Midlands £459
HF Holidays *Dovedale*
2299 Cycling and walking £349
HF Holidays *Freshwater Bay*
2300 Landscape painting £439
HF Holidays *Haytor, Devon*
2301 Birdwatching £364
HF Holidays *Isle of Arran*
2302 Landscape painting £439
HF Holidays *St Ives*

9–16 September
2303 Wildlife and other
fascinations of some
Hebridean islands £550
Univ Nottingham *Isle of Islay*

9–19 September
2304 Gourmet vegetarian
cookery £AFD
Acorn Activities *Scotland*

10–13 September
2305 Fine furniture making –
part 3 £AFD
West Dean College *Chichester*
ARCA

10–15 September
2306 Landscape painting £AFD
Acorn Activities *Pembrokeshire*

10–15 September
2307 Watercolour £AFD
Higham Hall *Cockermouth*
ARCA

September — Time to Learn

10–15 September
2308 Botanical illustration £AFD
2309 Printmaking workshop £AFD
West Dean College *Chichester*
ARCA

10–16 September
2310 Watercolour week £439
Watercolour Weeks at Weobley
Weobley, Hereford

11–15 September
2311 Gregorian music
for everyone £150
Ammerdown Centre *Radstock, Bath*

11–15 September
2312 Biological recording
techniques £200/250
Field Studies Council *Preston Montford, Shropshire*

11–15 September
2313 Country houses of
Sussex £AFD
Univ Birmingham *Brighton*

11–16 September
2314 Painting on china £AFD
2315 Monochrome photography
in the new millennium £AFD
Dillington House *Ilminster*
ARCA

11–17 September
2316 Walking the great
views £195/250
Field Studies Council *Castle Head Centre, Lake District*

12–16 September
2317 The theatre at Pitlochry £249
HF Holidays *Pitlochry*

14–17 September
2318 Herbs: their culinary,
cosmetic and medicinal
uses £112/144
Field Studies Council *Castle Head Centre, Lake District*

15–17 September
2319 Choral singing £90
2320 Miniature bookbinding £90
Alston Hall College *Preston*
ARCA

15–17 September
2321 Folk for fun £78/98
Belstead House *Ipswich*
ARCA

15–17 September
2322 String chamber music £AFD
Benslow Music Trust *Hitchin*
ARCA

15–17 September
2323 Happy go lucky English £110
Burton Manor College *Neston, Cheshire*
ARCA

15–17 September
2324 Portrait drawing for
beginners £158
2325 Mounting and framing
pictures £158
2326 Better swimming £158
2327 Tale telling £158
2328 Speak French –
elementary £158
2329 Introduction to the PC £188
The Earnley Concourse *Chichester, Sussex*

15–17 September
2330 The heroes journey £98/125
Field Studies Council *Castle Head Centre, Lake District*

15–17 September
2331 Early autumn birds: ringing and migration £89/114
2332 East Anglian vineyards and orchards £89/114
2333 Painting plants: early autumn colours £89/114
Field Studies Council *Flatford Mill, Essex*

15–17 September
2334 Four hands, one piano £105*
Jackdaws Educational Trust *Frome, Somerset*
food included. B & B extra

15–17 September
2335 History of the Royal Navy £107
2336 Meditation – to quieten the mind £107
2337 Flower painting £107
Knuston Hall *Irchester*
ARCA

15–17 September
2338 Weekend of healing for mind, body and spirit £AFD
2339 Internet for beginners £AFD
2340 French for absolute beginners £AFD
2341 Italian for absolute beginners £AFD
2342 Russian for absolute beginners £AFD
2343 Spanish for absolute beginners £AFD
2344 Greek for absolute beginners £AFD
Lancashire College *Chorley*
ARCA

15–17 September
2345 I wish I could paint – stage 2 £89/115
2346 The changing face of life on earth £89/115
Maryland College *Woburn*
ARCA

15–17 September
2347 Silversmithing and jewellery making £AFD
2348 Painting: wet in wet £AFD
2349 Close harmony and barbershop £AFD
The Old Rectory *Fittleworth*
ARCA

15–17 September
2350 German weekend £80/129
2351 Cromwell £80/129
Univ Cambridge *Madingley, Cambridge*

15–17 September
2352 Female deviance in early modern and modern England £125
2353 Goodbye to boiling oil: a new look at castles £145
2354 Sherlock Holmes and the Victorian detective £125
2355 Surfing the Internet £145
2356 The Celts £125
2357 Eastern philosophies £125
Univ Nottingham *Nottingham*

15–17 September
2358 History of watercolour painting £80
Wedgwood Memorial College *Barlaston*
ARCA

15–17 September
2359 Silk painting workshop £AFD
2360 Pottery for beginners £AFD
2361 Stained glass £AFD
2362 Lettercarving in stone and slate £AFD
2363 General silversmithing £AFD
2364 Making the most of your greenhouse £AFD
2365 Free machine embroidery £AFD
West Dean College *Chichester*
ARCA

15–18 September
2366 Painting flowers indoors £169
HF Holidays *Conistonwater*

15-18 September
2367 Country houses of Northumberland £AFD
Univ Liverpool *Newcastle*

15-22 September
2368 Painting and sketching: in Turner's footsteps £408
The Earnley Concourse *Chichester, Sussex*

15-22 September
2369 Insect week £226/290
2370 Insect photography week £243/312
Field Studies Council *Juniper Hall Centre, Dorking, Surrey*

16-17 September
2371 Decorative interiors and paint effects £AFD
Acorn Activities *Herefordshire*
2372 Pottery £AFD
2373 Stained glass £AFD
Acorn Activities *Scotland*

16-23 September
2374 Ballroom dancing – level 3 £344
HF Holidays *Conwy*
2375 Walking with Ceilidh dancing £319
HF Holidays *Isle of Arran*
2376 Photography tour £449
HF Holidays *St Ives*

17-21 September
2377 Pottery with other activities £AFD
Acorn Activities *Herefordshire*

17-21 September
2378 Stained glass workshop £180
Alston Hall College *Preston* ARCA

17-22 September
2379 Pastel painting £AFD
2380 Lakeside walks £AFD
Higham Hall *Cockermouth* ARCA

17-22 September
2381 Ironwork for the garden £AFD
2382 Painting the Sussex landscape £AFD
2383 Woodturning £AFD
2384 Pottery – glazes, glazing and firing £AFD
2385 Repair of books £AFD
West Dean College *Chichester* ARCA

17-23 September
2386 Painting the flowers of autumn £439
Watercolour Weeks at Weobley *Weobley, Hereford*

18-22 September
2387 Making traditional corn dollies £165
Ammerdown Centre *Radstock, Bath*

18-22 September
2388 Be adventurous with pastels £298
The Earnley Concourse *Chichester, Sussex*

18-22 September
2389 Modern pencil drawing £AFD
2390 Framing and mounting £AFD
2391 Follies and mad hatters £AFD
The Old Rectory *Fittleworth* ARCA

September — Time to Learn

18–23 September
2392 Painting – soft pastels outdoors £284
HF Holidays *Conistonwater*

19–22 September
2393 Music for pleasure £100
Wedgwood Memorial College *Barlaston*
ARCA

20–23 September
2394 Watercolour pencils £194
HF Holidays *Abingworth*

22–24 September
2395 Painting £90
2396 Enamelling £90
Alston Hall College *Preston*
ARCA

22–24 September
2397 A history of domestic things £78/98
2398 Portrait painting £78/98
2399 Creative writing £78/98
Belstead House *Ipswich*
ARCA

22–24 September
2400 Anyone can sing £115
Burton Manor College *Neston, Cheshire*
ARCA

22–24 September
2401 English folk dance £158
2402 Silk painting £158
2403 Bridge for improvers – level 1 £158
2404 Introduction to handwriting analysis £158
2405 Introduction to the Internet £188
The Earnley Concourse *Chichester, Sussex*

22–24 September
2406 Blencathra fungus weekend £85/115
Field Studies Council *Blencathra, Lake District*

22–24 September
2407 Have a go at canoeing £98/125
2408 Have a go at climbing £98/125
2409 Have a go at natural art £87/112
2410 Have a go at caving £98/125
Field Studies Council *Castle Head Centre, Lake District*

22–24 September
2411 Autumn walking weekend: three Suffolk estuaries £89/114
2412 Drawing and sketching for watercolour £89/114
2413 Wildlife illustration £89/114
2414 Exploring Suffolk and Essex villages £89/114
Field Studies Council *Flatford Mill, Essex*

22–24 September
2415 Drawing and painting for landscape £85/115
2416 Look out for mammals: an identification workshop £69/112
Field Studies Council *Preston Montford, Shropshire*

22–24 September
2417 Quilters' Guild £AFD
Higham Hall *Cockermouth*
ARCA

22–24 September
2418 Oratorio arias and ensembles £105*
Jackdaws Educational Trust *Frome, Somerset*
*food included. B & B extra

Wansfell College

Weekend and midweek adult residential courses in the beauty and seclusion of Epping Forest.

Our A-Z of subjects includes the Arts, Bridge, and Crafts; History, Literature and Music; Nature Studies, Photography, Wine Appreciation, and Yoga. Whether new to a subject or more experienced, you're bound to find a course to suit. Enjoy it in good company and pleasant surroundings.
Easy access via M25 or Tube.

For more information, including study tours, contact us at

**Theydon Bois, Epping,
Essex CM16 7LF
Tel: 01992 813027**

www.aredu.demon.co.uk/wansfellcollege
e-mail: Enrol@wansfell.demon.uk

ARCA

September — Time to Learn — September

22–24 September
2419 Bobbin lacemaking – mixed abilities £107
2420 Dowsing and divining £107
Knuston Hall *Irchester*
ARCA

22–24 September
2421 Open doors. A weekend for people with visual impairment £AFD
Lancashire College *Chorley*
ARCA

22–24 September
2422 Tai Chi £89/115
Maryland College *Woburn*
ARCA

22–24 September
2423 Creative plaster £AFD
2424 The wonderful world of fungi £AFD
2425 Atmosphere, mood and colour in watercolour £AFD
The Old Rectory *Fittleworth*
ARCA

22–24 September
2426 Chinese brush painting £AFD
Pendrell Hall College *Staffs*
ARCA

22–24 September
2427 Reading Greek £80/129
2428 Seen one, seen them all: film studies £80/129
2429 European popular woodcut print £80/129
Univ Cambridge *Madingley, Cambridge*

22–24 September
2430 Liverpool's heritage £150
Univ Nottingham *Liverpool*

2431 London's art galleries £175
Univ Nottingham *London*

22–24 September
2432 Bobbin lacemaking £AFD
2433 Watercolour painting £AFD
2434 Introduction to woodturning £AFD
2435 Drawing in pen, ink and pastel £AFD
2436 Photography in colour £AFD
West Dean College *Chichester*
ARCA

22–25 September
2437 Autumn nature photography £118/160
Field Studies Council *Preston Montford, Shropshire*

22–25 September
2438 Papermaking and painting with earth pigments £AFD
West Dean College *Chichester*
ARCA

23–24 September
2439 Sculpture £AFD
2440 Gourmet cookery £AFD
Acorn Activities *Herefordshire*
2441 Stone carving £AFD
Acorn Activities *Powys*
2442 Cookery for beginners £AFD
2443 Decorative interiors and paint effects £AFD
Acorn Activities *Scotland*
2444 Flower garden £AFD
Acorn Activities *Worcestershire*

23–24 September
2445 Forest spiders £32
Field Studies Council *Epping Forest Centre, Essex*

September   *Time to Learn*   September

23–27 September
2446 Map and compass £221
HF Holidays *Alnmouth*
2447 Elgar revisited £189
HF Holidays *Freshwater Bay*
2448 Island tour on a bike £174
HF Holidays *Isle of Arran*
2449 Health and wellbeing £249
HF Holidays *Malhamdale*
2450 Whisky trail £199
HF Holidays *Pitlochry*

23–30 September
2451 North Wales Music Festival £424
2452 Folk dancing for all £374
HF Holidays *Brecon*
2453 North Wales music £424
HF Holidays *Conwy*
2454 Bridge and sightseeing £409
HF Holidays *St Ives*
2455 Scottish country dancing – level 3 £379
HF Holidays *Whitby*

24–26 September
2456 Developing self £95
Alston Hall College *Preston* ARCA

24–27 September
2457 Framing workshop £AFD
West Dean College *Chichester* ARCA

24–28 September
2458 Drawing and painting on silk £AFD
2459 Creative photography £AFD
West Dean College *Chichester* ARCA

24–29 September
2460 Landscape painting £AFD
Higham Hall *Cockermouth* ARCA

24–29 September
2461 Stone sculpture £AFD
West Dean College *Chichester* ARCA

24–30 September
2462 Watercolour week £439
Watercolour Weeks at Weobley *Weobley, Hereford*

24–30 September
2463 Country chairmaking £AFD
West Dean College *Chichester* ARCA

25–27 September
2464 Paintings of the National Portrait Gallery £90
Alston Hall College *Preston* ARCA

25–28 September
2465 Group quartet workshop £AFD
Benslow Music Trust *Hitchin* ARCA

25–29 September
2466 Tapestry weaving £145
2467 Card-making £145
Ammerdown Centre *Radstock, Bath*

25–29 September
2468 Honiton lacemaking £AFD
Urchfont Manor College *Devizes* ARCA

26–30 September
2469 The theatre at Pitlochry £249
HF Holidays *Pitlochry*

Time to Learn

27–29 September
2470 Life drawing — £100
Alston Hall College *Preston*
ARCA

27–30 September
2471 The English opera — £139
HF Holidays *Freshwater Bay*
2472 Writing for money — £179
HF Holidays *Malhamdale*

28–30 September
2473 Aspects of antiques — £78/98
2474 Cromwell, our chief of men — £78/98
Belstead House *Ipswich*
ARCA

28 September–1 October
2475 Fungus foray — £110/138
Field Studies Council *Nettlecombe Court Centre, Exmoor*

29–31 September
2476 Late Gothic illuminated manuscripts — £80/129
2477 Bede to Beowulf — £80/129
2478 C20th British musicals — £80/129
Univ Cambridge *Madingley, Cambridge*

29 September–1 October
2479 Embroidered fabric covered boxes — £90
2480 Counselling level I — £90
2481 Alexander Technique – introduction — £95
Alston Hall College *Preston*
ARCA

29 September–1 October
2482 Creative fun for grown-up children — £75
Ammerdown Centre *Radstock, Bath*

29 September–1 October
2483 Colour mixing for beginners — £158
2484 Miniature painting for beginners — £158
2485 Film history: more British studios — £158
2486 Using your PC — £188
The Earnley Concourse *Chichester, Sussex*

29 September–1 October
2487 Birds, beasts and bugs: exploring animal biodiversity — £89/114
2488 Managing wetlands for wildlife — £93/119
2489 Improve your watercolours — £89/114
2490 Botanical illustration for improvers — £89/114
2491 Suffolk's medieval churches — £89/114
Field Studies Council *Flatford Mill, Essex*

29 September–1 October
2492 Look out for mammals: an identification workshop — £69/112
Field Studies Council *Nettlecombe Court Centre, Exmoor*

29 September–1 October
2493 Silver workshop — £AFD
Higham Hall *Cockermouth*
ARCA

September — Time to Learn — September

29 September–1 October

2494	Christmas crafts	£107
2495	The Cold War	£107
2496	Trousers that fit	£107
2497	An introduction to churchyard lichens	£107

Knuston Hall *Irchester*
ARCA

29 September–1 October

2498	Arts and crafts for fund-raisers	£AFD
2499	Tai Chi for beginners	£AFD
2500	Spreadsheets – an introduction to MS EXCEL	£AFD
2501	German	£AFD

Lancashire College *Chorley*
ARCA

29 September–1 October

2502	Turner and Constable	£89/115
2503	Belgian lace making	£89/115

Maryland College *Woburn*
ARCA

29 September–1 October

2504	Fiction writing: character, dialogue and atmosphere	£AFD
2505	Calligraphy: introducing/revising the Carolingian miniscule script	£AFD
2506	Exploring Roman Sussex	£AFD
2507	Pastels in autumn	£AFD

The Old Rectory *Fittleworth*
ARCA

29 September–1 October

2508	Archaeology of the Peak District: the White Peak	£120

Univ Nottingham *Cromford*

29 September–1 October

2509	Mushrooms and toadstools	£AFD

Urchfont Manor College *Devizes*
ARCA

29 September–1 October

2510	An introduction to mosaic	£AFD
2511	Jewellery making	£AFD
2512	Ink flower painting – handling colour	£AFD
2513	Glass engraving – botanical subjects	£AFD
2514	Drawing and watercolour painting	£AFD

West Dean College *Chichester*
ARCA

30 September–1 October

2515	Glass making and blowing	£AFD
2516	Photography	£AFD
2517	Drawing for the terrified	£AFD
2518	Pottery	£AFD

Acorn Activities *Herefordshire*

2519	Mosaic	£AFD

Acorn Activities *Scotland*

2520	Garden design	£AFD

Acorn Activities *Worcestershire*

30 September–4 October

2521	Brush up your Acol	£214

HF Holidays *Bourton-on-the-Water*

2522	Literary Lakeland	£264

HF Holidays *Derwentwater*

2523	Painting trees	£244

HF Holidays *Malhamdale*

30 September–6 October

2524	Painting boats and harbours	£369

HF Holidays *Alnmouth*

2525	Walking with Ceilidh dancing	£379

HF Holidays *Brecon*

2526 Birthplace of the canals £309
HF Holidays *Dovedale*
2527 Belly dancing £289
HF Holidays *Freshwater Bay*

2528 Geology of Arran £344
HF Holidays *Isle of Arran*
2529 Scottish dancing and walking – level 3 £349
HF Holidays *Pitlochry*

Study Tours and Learning Holidays Abroad

April 2000

April

Italian language
2530 Standard beginners (40 hours) £255
2531 Intensive beginners (80 hours) £475
2532 Intermediate/advanced (60 hours) £370
2533 Michaelangelo and his influence – 2 weeks £190
2534 Art in Florence – 1 week £230
2535 Drawing – 3 weeks £135
2536 Cooking – 3 weeks £110

British Institute of Florence *Italy*
Accommodation arranged in Florentine homes or pensioni

1–8 April
2537 Painting £495
2538 Walking in the Charente £450
2539 French for Francophiles £520

L'Age Baston Holidays *La Rochefoucauld, France*

4–9 April
2540 Modern art in New York £660

Univ Birmingham *New York*

8–15 April
2541 Getting into journalism £450

Charente Activity Centre *Aubeterre-sur-Dronne, France*

8–15 April
2542 Painting £495
2543 Walking in the Charente £450
2544 French for Francophiles £520

L'Age Baston Holidays *La Rochefoucauld, France*

8–22 April
2545 Flowers of Andalucia: Serranía de Ronda and Costa de la Luz £1420

Field Studies Council Overseas *Andalucia, Spain*

11–25 April
2546 Crete through the artist's eye: sketching, painting, walking and spring flowers £1500

Field Studies Council Overseas *Crete, Greece*

12–19 April
2547 Cyprus: rocks and flowers £690

Univ Nottingham *Paphos, Cyprus*

15–22 April
2548 Painting £495
2549 French country cooking £495
2550 French for Francophiles £520

L'Age Baston Holidays *La Rochefoucauld, France*

April   *Time to Learn*   **May**

15–25 April
2551 Archaeology of the Holy Land £1520
Univ Nottingham *Jerusalem and Tiberias*

16–29 April
2552 Tambopata: a wildlife El Dorado in Peru £2000
Field Studies Council Overseas *Peru*

19–28 April
2553 Easter on Guernsey: flowers and landscapes in the Channel Islands £790
Field Studies Council Overseas *Guernsey*

22–29 April
2554 Irish language at all levels £115
2555 Cultural hillwalking £95
Oideas Gael *County Donegal, Southern Ireland*

22–30 April
2556 Painting £495
2557 French for Francophiles £520
2558 Walking in the Charente £450
L'Age Baston Holidays *La Rochefoucauld, France*

28 April–6 May
2559 Ice cold in Svalbard: an Arctic archipelago in spring £2000
Field Studies Council Overseas *Svalbard, Norway*

29 April–6 May
2560 Open painting week (untutored) £275
Charente Activity Centre *Aubeterre-sur-Dronne, France*

■ ■ ■ ■

May 2000

☐ ☐ ☐ ☐

May
    Italian language
2561 Standard beginners (40 hours) £255
2562 Intensive beginners (80 hours) £475
2563 Intermediate/advanced (60 hours) £370
2564 Florentine Renaissance – 4 weeks £240
2565 Brunelleschi – 3 days £115
2566 Drawing – 4 weeks £135
2567 Landscape watercolours – 2 weeks £135
2568 Cooking – 4 weeks £110
2569 Dante – 1 week £90
2570 Opera – 2 weeks £90
British Institute of Florence *Italy Accommodation arranged in Florentine homes or pensioni*

4–16 May
2571 Pilgrimage to Santiago de Compostela £1320
Univ Birmingham *Spain*

6–13 May
2572 Painting £495
2573 Walking in the Charente £450
L'Age Baston Holidays *La Rochefoucauld, France*

May — Time to Learn

6–13 May
2574 Form in 3D sculpture £350
Charente Activity Centre *Aubeterre-sur-Dronne, France*

7–21 May
2575 Painting in Greece £1200
Field Studies Council Overseas *Parga, Greece*

11–27 May
2576 Wildlife of an Iberian river: the Ebro from source to sea £1800
Field Studies Council Overseas *Spain*

13–19 May
2577 Gardens of south-west Ireland £600
Univ Nottingham *Eire*

13–20 May
2578 Painting £495
2579 Walking in the Charente £450
L'Age Baston Holidays *La Rochefoucauld, France*

13–20 May
2580 Painting – colour and landscape £350
Charente Activity Centre *Aubeterre-sur-Dronne, France*

20–27 May
2581 Painting £495
2582 French for Francophiles £520
2583 Walking in the Charente £450
L'Age Baston Holidays *La Rochefoucauld, France*

20–27 May
2584 Travel writing £450
Charente Activity Centre *Aubeterre-sur-Dronne, France*

20–27 May
2585 Relaxology (relaxation) £195*
2586 Light, landscape and myth (art) £195*
2587 Walking £195*
The Greek Experience *Kythira, Greece*
tuition only

20–27 May
2588 Prague Spring Music Festival £680
Univ Nottingham *Prague, Czech Republic*

22–27 May
2589 Cracow: the art treasury of Poland £775
Univ Birmingham *Cracow, Poland*

22 May–5 June
2590 Paloponnese: the world of the Myceneans £1340
Univ Nottingham *Greece*

27 May–3 June
2591 Painting £495
2592 Walking in the Charente £450
2593 French for Francophiles £520
L'Age Baston Holidays *La Rochefoucauld, France*

27 May–3 June
2594 Greek language (level 2/3) £195*
2595 Images of an island (art) £195*
2596 Healthy mind, healthy body (yoga) £195*
The Greek Experience *Kythira, Greece*
tuition only

27 May–6 June
2597 Danube delta: wild wetlands of Romania £1250
Field Studies Council Overseas *Romania*

LES ARTS VIVANTS

RESIDENTIAL COURSES AND STUDY TOURS
JUNE – SEPTEMBER 2000

Architecture, Interiors, Gardens, Pre-historic Art, Textiles, Dance and Drama taught in English at the seventeenth century CHÂTEAU MONFERRIER a unique historical setting in the Dordogne region of South West France with fifty acres of park and woodland, large swimming pool and tennis court

Write, Phone or Fax for Brochures:

**Sally Bowden, Course Director,
Les Arts Vivants SARL
Château Monferrier**
24330 St. Pierre de Chignac, France.

Tel. (33) 5 05 53 06 75 36   Fax: (33) 5 05 53 06 08 82

Expanding your horizons

L'Age Baston Holidays

Painting & Drawing
French for Francophiles
Walking in the Charente
French Country Cooking

Qualified professional tuition
Wonderful accommodation, superb food.
Relaxed and friendly atmosphere

Alexandra & John Waddington
Château L'Age Baston
16110 St Projet St Constant
La Rochefoucauld
France

Tel: (0033)5456 35307
Fax: (0033) 5456 30903
e-mail: LageBaston@aol.com

The Greek Experience

on the unspoilt island of Kythira

Art, Circle Dance, Greek Folk Dance, Greek Language, Massage, Photography, Relaxation, Walking, Writing, Personal Development and much more

For further information and full programme telephone

02392 830312

Web:www.greekexperience.com

"like staying with friends"

| May | *Time to Learn* | June |

28 May–4 June
2598 French £452*
Brasshouse Language Courses
Brittany, France
*includes transport

28 May–4 June
2599 From eye to creation – painting abstract or realism £350
Charente Activity Centre *Aubeterre-sur-Dronne, France*

29 May–4 June
2600 Art and architecture in Holland £660
Univ Nottingham *Delft and Amsterdam, Holland*

31 May–14 June
2601 Sierra Nevada to Death Valley: ecology and geology in California £2200
Field Studies Council Overseas *California, USA*

■ ■ ■ ■

June 2000

☐ ☐ ☐ ☐

June
Italian language
2602 Standard beginners (40 hours) £255
2603 Intensive beginners (80 hours) £475
2604 Intermediate/advanced (60 hours) £370
2605 High Renaissance and beyond – 4 weeks £240
2606 Florentine palaces – 3 days £115
2607 Drawing – 4 weeks £135
2608 Landscape watercolours – 2 weeks £135
2609 Cooking – 4 weeks £110
British Institute of Florence *Italy*
Accommodation arranged in Florentine homes or pensioni

1–15 June
2610 Picos de Europa: exploring one of Europe's last wildlife refuges £1650
Field Studies Council Overseas *Northern Spain*

2–5 June
2611 Irish language £55
2612 Cultural hillwalking £45
2613 Bodhrán playing £50
Oideas Gael *County Donegal, Southern Ireland*

3–10 June
2614 Painting £495
2615 Walking in the Charente £450
L'Age Baston Holidays *La Rochefoucauld, France*

3–10 June
2616 Greek language (level 2/3) £195*
2617 Images of an island (art) £195*
2618 Walking £195*
The Greek Experience *Kythira, Greece*
*tuition only

3–10 June
2619 Normandy: medieval to modern £AFD
Univ Birmingham *Normandy*

143

Time to Learn

7–17 June
2620 Early summer in
Andalucia: southern
Spain and Doñana
National Park £1370
Field Studies Council Overseas *Andalucia, Spain*

7–22 June
2621 Land of the golden
fleece: Georgian
churches and flowers
of the Caucasus £2000
Field Studies Council Overseas *Georgia*

9–11 June
2622 Wildlife weekend £AFD
Acorn Activities *Jersey*

10–17 June
2623 Painting £495
2624 Walking in the Charente £450
L'Age Baston Holidays *La Rochefoucauld, France*

10–17 June
2625 Greek language
(level 3/4) £195*
2626 Images of an island
(art) £195*
2627 Writing novels and
stories £195*
The Greek Experience *Kythira, Greece*
*tuition only

10–17 June
2628 Irish language £115
Oideas Gael *County Donegal, Southern Ireland*

11–17 June
2629 Gardens and interiors:
discovering the
Dordogne £400
Les Arts Vivants *St Pierre de Chignac, France*

17–24 June
2630 Painting £495
2631 Walking in the Charente £450
2632 French for Francophiles £520
L'Age Baston Holidays *La Rochefoucauld, France*

17–24 June
2633 Traditional methods
of stone carving £375
Charente Activity Centre *Aubeterre-sur-Dronne, France*

17–24 June
2634 Writing: finding
your voice £195*
2635 Images of an island
(art) £195*
2636 Photography: live form
and creativity £195*
The Greek Experience *Kythira, Greece*
*tuition only

17–24 June
2637 Irish language £115
Oideas Gael *County Donegal, Southern Ireland*

19–26 June
2638 Study tour to the
Wadden-Sea
(Friesian Islands,
Germany) £310*
Univ Wales Swansea *Germany*
*not including transport to Germany

22 June–6 July
2639 Carpathian landscapes:
geology, natural history
and castles in Romania £1650
Field Studies Council Overseas *Romania*

24 June–1 July
2640 Painting £495
2641 Walking in the Charente £450
2642 French for Francophiles £520
L'Age Baston Holidays *La Rochefoucauld, France*

| June | Time to Learn | July |

24 June–1 July
2643 Scriptwriting: creating theatre £195*
2644 Light, landscape and myth (art) £195*
2645 Success from setbacks (personal development) £195*
The Greek Experience *Kythira, Greece*
*tuition only

24 June–1 July
2646 Irish language £115
Oideas Gael *County Donegal, Southern Ireland*

25 June–1 July
2647 Knot gardens, topiary and tapestry: discovering the Dordogne £400
Les Arts Vivants *St Pierre de Chignac, France*

28 June–4 July
2648 Irish studies £460
Summer Academy *Univ College Cork, Ireland*

■ ■ ■ ■

July 2000

☐ ☐ ☐ ☐

July
Italian language
2649 Standard beginners (40 hours) £255
2650 Intensive beginners (80 hours) £475
2651 Intermediate/advanced (60 hours) £370
2652 Florentine Renaissance – 4 weeks £240
2653 Art in Florence – 1 week £230
2654 Drawing – 4 weeks £135
2655 Cooking – 4 weeks £110
British Institute of Florence *Italy*
Accommodation arranged in Florentine homes or pensioni

1–8 July
2656 Painting £495
2657 Walking in the Charente £450
2658 French for Francophiles £520
L'Age Baston Holidays *La Rochefoucauld, France*

1–8 July
2659 Irish language £115
2660 Celtic pottery £95
2661 Environment and culture £95
Oideas Gael *County Donegal, Southern Ireland*

5–11 July
2662 Celtic civilization £460
Summer Academy *Univ College Cork, Ireland*

6–16 July
2663 The Bernese Oberland: mountain flowers and walking £1350
Field Studies Council Overseas *Switzerland*

8–15 July
2664 Painting £495
2665 Walking in the Charente £450
2666 French for Francophiles £520
L'Age Baston Holidays *La Rochefoucauld, France*

July — Time to Learn

8–15 July
2667 Flowers of the Burren: Ireland's botanical enigma £790
Field Studies Council Overseas *Co. Clare, Ireland*

8–15 July
2668 Irish language £115
2669 Cultural hillwalking £95
Oideas Gael *County Donegal, Southern Ireland*

8–15 July
2670 Warsaw Mozart Festival £740
Univ Nottingham *Poland*

9–15 July
2671 Gardens and interiors: discovering the Dordogne £400
Les Arts Vivants *St Pierre de Chignac, France*

12–18 July
2672 The folklore and cultural heritage of Ireland £460
Summer Academy *Univ College Cork, Ireland*

15–22 July
2673 Painting £495
2674 Walking in the Charente £450
2675 French for Francophiles £520
L'Age Baston Holidays *La Rochefoucauld, France*

15–22 July
2676 Irish language £115
2677 Cultural hillwalking £95
2678 Flute playing £95
Oideas Gael *County Donegal, Southern Ireland*

16–23 July
2679 The high valleys of Andorra: flowers and painting £970
Field Studies Council Overseas *Andorra, Pyrenees*

22–29 July
2680 Painting £495
2681 Walking in the Charente £450
2682 French for Francophiles £520
L'Age Baston Holidays *La Rochefoucauld, France*

22–29 July
2683 Summer school in Irish language and culture £125
Oideas Gael *County Donegal, Southern Ireland*

22 July–5 August
2684 Cuba libre: an intoxicating cocktail of wildlife, history and culture £1950
Field Studies Council Overseas *Cuba*

23–29 July
2685 Knot gardens, topiary and tapestry: discovering the Dordogne £400
Les Arts Vivants *St Pierre de Chignac, France*

23–30 July
2686 The Camargue and its environs: dragonflies and birds of the Rhône delta £980
Field Studies Council Overseas *Camargue, Southern France*

July   *Time to Learn*   August

29 July–5 August
2687 Irish language £115
2688 Archaeology summer school £95
Oideas Gael *County Donegal, Southern Ireland*

31 July–5 August
2689 Painting £495
2690 French country cooking £495
2691 French for Francophiles £520
L'Age Baston Holidays *La Rochefoucauld, France*

August 2000

August
2692 Italian language – all levels £280
2693 Opera – 1 week £90
British Institute of Florence *Italy*
Accommodation arranged in homes or pensioni. During August the Institute moves to the Tuscan coast at Massa

5–12 August
2694 Painting £495
2695 Walking in the Charente £450
2696 French for Francophiles £520
L'Age Baston Holidays *La Rochefoucauld, France*

5–12 August
2697 Irish language £115
2698 Cultural hillwalking £95
Oideas Gael *County Donegal, Southern Ireland*

5–13 August
2699 In the steps of the Plantagenets: medieval castles and abbeys in the Loire valley £740
Univ Nottingham *Loire Valley, France*

6–13 August
2700 Dances of 17th and 18th centuries £340
Les Arts Vivants *St Pierre de Chignac, France*

12–19 August
2701 Painting £495
2702 Walking in the Charente £450
2703 French for Francophiles £520
L'Age Baston Holidays *La Rochefoucauld, France*

12–19 August
2704 Irish language £115
2705 Cultural hillwalking £95
Oideas Gael *County Donegal, Southern Ireland*

17–24 August
2706 Sing your dance, dance your song (circle dance) £195*
2707 Greek folk dance £195*
The Greek Experience *Kythira, Greece*
tuition only

19–26 August
2708 Painting £495
2709 Walking in the Charente £450
2710 French for Francophiles £520
L'Age Baston Holidays *La Rochefoucauld, France*

19–26 August
2711 Irish language £115
2712 Dances of Ireland £90
Oideas Gael *County Donegal, Southern Ireland*

The Charente Activity Centre

Le Poulailler or as it's known locally "the meeting place of the deer" is home to The Charente Activity Centre. The Perigordian farmhouse set in 14 acres of rolling countryside in south west France provides the perfect setting for a relaxed and creative holiday.

Like to have a new hobby?

- Stone Carving
- Sculpture
- Landscape Painting
- Impressionism
- Pastels
- Cave Painting
- Travel Writing
- Journalism

Want to polish up an old skill?

Join one of our small friendly groups for excellent tuition and good food & wine. Non-participating partners will find plenty to do in this beautiful area, 2km from Aubeterre-sur-Dronne (un des plus beaux villages de France) easy access by Eurostar & TGV

For further details write, phone or fax:
The Charente Activity Centre
"Le Poulailler", 16210 St. Romain, France
Tel/fax: (+33) 5 45 98 63 92
www.arthouse.uk.com/artfrance.htm

THE BRITISH INSTITUTE OF FLORENCE

- Two and four week courses of Italian at various levels
- Also Art History, Opera, Drawing, Cooking, Dante, Landscape Watercolours
- Art History 'mini breaks' lasting from three to eight days
- Excellent study facilities in the Harold Acton library
- Accommodation found in Florentine homes or pensioni
- Summer courses in characteristic medieval hill town
- Tailor-made programmes organised for individuals and groups

Full details from:
The British Institute of Florence
Piazza Strozzi 2, 50123 Firenze, Italy
Tel: 0039 055 26778200
Fax: 0039 055 26778222
Email:info@britishinstitute.it
Web:www.britishinstitute.it

IRISH LANGUAGE AND CULTURE

Irish Courses for Adults at all learning levels

Also Cultural Courses in

Set-Dancing
Painting
Archaeology
Hillwalking
Weaving
Pottery
Environment
Bodhrán

Brochure
OIDEAS GAEL
Glenn Cholm Cille
Co Dhún na nGall
Éire

Phone: 00-353-73-30248
Fax: 00-353-73-30348
EMail:oidsgael@iol.ie
www.Oideas-Gael.com

| August | *Time to Learn* | September |

19–28 August
2713 Wildlife of the
central Pyrenees £590
Univ Nottingham *Jaca, Spain*

20–26 August
2714 Weaving and spinning £400
Les Arts Vivants *St Pierre de Chignac, France*

22 August–7 September
2715 A foray through
Ussuriland: the
secret world of the
Russian far east £2950
Field Studies Council Overseas
Ussuriland, Russia

26 August–2 September
2716 Painting £495
2717 Walking in the Charente £450
2718 French for Francophiles £520
L'Age Baston Holidays
La Rochefoucauld, France

26 August–2 September
2719 Art & Architecture in
Tuscan & Umbrian
Hill towns £870
Univ Nottingham *Italy*

1–10 September
2720 Architecture & Art of
Boston, Massachusetts £960
Univ Nottingham *Boston, USA*

■ ■ ■ ■

September 2000

☐ ☐ ☐ ☐

September
    Italian language
2721 Standard beginners
(40 hours) £255
2722 Intensive beginners
(80 hours) £475
2723 Intermediate/advanced
(60 hours) £370
2724 Michaelangelo and
his influence – 3 weeks £190
2725 Art in Florence – 1 week £230
2726 Drawing – 4 weeks £135
2727 Cooking – 3 weeks £110
2728 Dante – 5 days £90
2729 Opera – 2 weeks £90
British Institute of Florence *Italy*
Accommodation arranged in Florentine homes or pensioni

Late September/October
    Italian language
2730 Standard beginners
(40 hours) £255
2731 Intensive beginners
(80 hours) £475
2732 Intermediate/advanced
(60 hours) £370
2733 Florentine Renaissance –
4 weeks £240
2734 Villas and gardens –
5 days £225
2735 Drawing – 4 weeks £135
2736 Cooking – 4 weeks £110
2737 Dante – 5 days £90
2738 Opera – 5 days £90
British Institute of Florence *Italy*
Accommodation arranged in Florentine homes or pensioni

September
2739 Study tour to the
Pyrenees £AFD
Univ Wales Swansea *Pyrenees*

September — Time to Learn — September

2–9 September
2740 Painting £495
2741 Walking in the Charente £450
2742 French for Francophiles £520
L'Age Baston Holidays *La Rochefoucauld, France*

2–9 September
2743 Travel writing £450
Charente Activity Centre *Aubeterre-sur-Dronne, France*

2–9 September
2744 Practical ecology in Poland: mammals of the Bialowieza Forest £940
Field Studies Council Overseas *Poland*

2–9 September
2745 The hero's journey (personal development) £195*
2746 Greek language level 3/4 £195*
2747 Photography: creating dramatic images £195*
The Greek Experience *Kythira, Greece*
*tuition only

2–9 September
2748 Imperial Rome £AFD
Univ Birmingham *Rome*

3–9 September
2749 Caves and castles: discovering the Dordogne £400
Les Arts Vivants *St Pierre de Chignac, France*

8–10 September
2750 Cultural hillwalking £35
2751 Bodhrán playing £35
Oideas Gael *County Donegal, Southern Ireland*

9–16 September
2752 Painting £495
2753 Walking in the Charente £450
2754 French for Francophiles £520
L'Age Baston Holidays *La Rochefoucauld, France*

9–16 September
2755 Writing: the popular muse £195*
2756 Holistic massage £195*
2757 Walking £195*
The Greek Experience *Kythira, Greece*
*tuition only
2758 The Rock of Gibraltar: bird migration £830
Univ Nottingham *Gibraltar*

11 September–2 October
2759 An African safari: Kalahari and Okavango £3200
Univ Nottingham *Botswana*

13–29 September
2760 The land below the wind: rainforests, people and wildlife of Sabah £3200
Field Studies Council Overseas *Sabah, Malaysia*

15–17 September
2761 Wildlife weekend £AFD
Acorn Activities *Jersey*

16–23 September
2762 Painting £495
2763 Walking in the Charente £450
2764 French for Francophiles £520
L'Age Baston Holidays *La Rochefoucauld, France*

16–23 September
2765 Greek folk dance £195*
The Greek Experience *Kythira, Greece*
*tuition only

September — Time to Learn

17–23 September
2766 Caves and castles: discovering the Dordogne £400
Les Arts Vivants *St Pierre de Chignac, France*

17 September–3 October
2767 From Karoo to Fynbos: the ecology of South Africa's western cape £2950
Field Studies Council Overseas *South Africa*

23–30 September
2768 Painting £495
2769 French country cooking £495
2770 French for Francophiles £520
L'Age Baston Holidays *La Rochefoucauld, France*

23–30 September
2771 Sundancer (circle dance) £195*
The Greek Experience *Kythira, Greece*
tuition only

25 September–5th October
2772 Autumn in Andalucia: southern Spain and Doñana National Park £1370
Field Studies Council Overseas *Andalucia, Spain*

30 September–7th October
2773 Painting £495
2774 French country cooking £495
2775 French for Francophiles £520
L'Age Baston Holidays *La Rochefoucauld, France*

30 September–7 October
2776 Greek language levels 2/3/4 £195*
2777 Images of an island (art) £195*
2778 Walking £195*
The Greek Experience *Kythira, Greece*
tuition only

30 September–7 October
2779 Medieval Istanbul £790
Univ Nottingham *Istanbul*

ORDER FORM

April 2000 – September 2000

Published January 2000

price £4.95 post free in UK
(Overseas airmail £8.00; Overseas surface mail £6.50 sterling)

Please send me .... copy/copies of
TIME TO LEARN April 2000 – September 2000

☐ Payment of £ .... enclosed (cheques payable to NIACE)
☐ Please debit my credit card (Visa, Delta, Mastercard, Eurocard) number

☐☐☐☐ ☐☐☐☐ ☐☐☐☐ ☐☐☐☐

Expiry date: ☐☐ ☐☐

Send with payment to:
Publications Sales, NIACE
21 De Montfort Street, Leicester LE1 7GE

OR, take this completed form to your bookseller to order on your behalf

Name: _____

Address: _____

_____

_____

_____

Trade orders to: Central Books Ltd., 99 Wallis Road, London E9 5LN
Tel: 0181 986 4854; Fax: 0181 533 5821

Time to Learn

ENQUIRY COUPON

To find out more about a learning holiday you have seen listed in this book, complete this coupon and send it DIRECT to the Organiser. Please do not send it to NIACE.

Please send me further information on the following learning holiday(s) as advertised by you in *Time to Learn*.

_____

_____

_____

_____

Please fill in your name and address on the reverse side ▶

ENQUIRY COUPON

To find out more about a learning holiday you have seen listed in this book, complete this coupon and send it DIRECT to the Organiser. Please do not send it to NIACE.

Please send me further information on the following learning holiday(s) as advertised by you in *Time to Learn*.

_____

_____

_____

_____

Please fill in your name and address on the reverse side ▶

ENQUIRY COUPON

To find out more about a learning holiday you have seen listed in this book, complete this coupon and send it DIRECT to the Organiser. Please do not send it to NIACE.

Please send me further information on the following learning holiday(s) as advertised by you in *Time to Learn*.

_____

_____

_____

_____

Please fill in your name and address on the reverse side ▶

Name:
Address:
Postcode:

Name:
Address:
Postcode:

Name:
Address:
Postcode:

Subject Index

The numbers listed in this index refer to the individual numbers assigned to each learning holiday: ***they are not page numbers.*** To guide you, the learning holidays numbered from 1 to 352 are being held during April 2000; 353 to 753 during May 2000; 754 to 1240 in June 2000; 1241 to 1743 in July 2000; 1744 to 2162 in August 2000 and 2163 to 2529 in September 2000. Numbers 2530 to 2779 cover learning holidays and study tours abroad.

3D découpage 691
Absolute beginners 1376, 1746
Acol, Brush up your 2521
Adventure activities 1642, 1722, 1722, 1810, 2065
Africa 2759
Age of Enlightenment, the 1502
Ageing and retirement 103, 858
Alberni masterclass 254, 1537
Alexander Technique 173, 347, 420, 1098, 1101, 1139, 2259, 2481
Alexander the Great 1989
Alfred the Great 1709
America, history of 1125, 1504
American Indians 692, 2173
Andalucia 2545, 2620, 2772
Andorra 2679
Anglo-Saxons, the 1085
Antiques 1131, 1265, 1394, 2044, 2473
Archaeology 567, 613, 690, 1021, 1166, 1359, 1462, 1533, 2041, 2104, 2508, 2688
Architecture 357, 818, 1091, 1222, 1338, 1442, 1583, 1620, 1847, 2238
Aromatherapy 271, 834, 1466
Arran, Isle of 1054
Art and craft 208, 237, 411, 616, 742, 755, 1836, 2387, 2467, 2482, 2494, 2498
Art appreciation 155, 174, 533, 562, 657, 987, 1129, 1213, 1262, 1314, 1392, 1505, 1588, 1597, 1603, 1798, 2020, 2137, 2280, 2358, 2431, 2464, 2502, 2605
Art in Florence 2534, 2653, 2725
Art 302, 831, 901, 1079, 1203, 1219, 1381, 1723, 1754, 1781, 1868, 2106, 2154, 2409, 2586, 2617, 2626, 2635, 2644, 2777
Asia 2188

Astrology 382
Astronomy 116, 393, 475, 1891, 2254
Audiovisual presentations 817
Auschwitz 820
Austen, Jane 694, 920, 1315, 1455, 2072
Bach, J.S. 29, 34, 1653, 2179
Badger, the 588
Banjo, the 1772
Basketry 138, 484, 1060, 1993
Bassoon, the 1983
Batik 169, 453, 825, 1135, 1473, 1790, 2278
Bats 1093, 1775, 1975, 2159
Bead needle weaving: C&G 611, 1107
Beadwork 670, 1409, 1615, 1779, 2058
Beckett, Samuel 788, 814
Beethoven, Ludwig van 47, 1100
Bell ringing 1501
Bernese Oberland, the 2663
Bird songs and calls 390, 490, 491, 572, 781, 1048
Birdwatching 134, 153, 229, 247, 262, 287, 342, 441, 472, 519, 528, 547, 704, 713, 719, 779, 845, 855, 990, 1157, 1403, 1665, 1795, 2108, 2126, 2208, 2222, 2301, 2331
Black death, the 156
Blacksmithing 100, 168, 508, 729, 824, 1228, 1551, 1829
Bodhrán, the 2613, 2751
Bookcraft 32, 250, 356, 628, 844, 853, 1240, 1486, 1617, 2320, 2385
Botanical illustration 17, 42, 180, 810, 902, 957, 1031, 1069, 1312, 1363, 1633, 1897, 1931, 1948, 2071, 2102, 2107, 2176, 2308, 2490
Botany 2253
Bowls 440, 848, 942, 1558
Brass instruments 2134

Bridge and sightseeing 1053, 1255, 1342, 2125, 2296, 2454
Bridge and walking 947, 1696, 1856
Bridge 12, 85, 92, 105, 113, 114, 190, 191, 227, 233, 248, 286, 345, 351, 481, 699, 764, 766, 793, 899, 909, 1087, 1177, 1425, 1601, 2019, 2076, 2097, 2177, 2262, 2403
Bridgemaking 198
Britain, history of 231, 317, 497, 687, 1464, 1867, 2129
British monarchy, the 1461
British Sign Language 867
Brontës, the 922, 2293
Bronze Age, the 595
Brunelleschi, Fillippo 2565
Business studies 324, 1651, 1988
Butterflies and moths 709, 1300, 1422, 1522, 1735, 1876, 1899, 1958, 1960
Byron, George Gordon 1115
Cabinet making 75, 654, 1884, 2229
California 2601
Calligraphy: 9, 55, 61, 111, 145, 151, 203, 239, 380, 466, 524, 797, 1033, 1136, 1142, 1239, 1379, 1479, 1529, 1606, 1666, 1742, 1863, 2050, 2088, 2135, 2198, 2234, 2268, 2505
Camargue, the 2686
Camcorder and video 1437, 1984
Canal boat art 280, 304
Canals 199, 2526
Cane, rush and willow work 341, 448, 522, 1032, 1145, 1330, 1639, 2139
Canoeing 2407
Canvas work 309
Caring for the carer 2186
Castles 862, 943, 1209, 1851, 2011, 2043, 2353, 2699
Caucasus, the 2621
Caving 2410
Cello, the 49, 672, 887
Celts, the 140, 731, 1953, 2356, 2660, 2662
Ceramics 166, 1388, 1552, 1621, 1634, 1690, 1759, 1947
Cézanne 1225
Chair making 2169, 2463
Chichester 455
China painting 122, 279, 461, 556, 1512, 1650, 1822, 2314

China restoration 266, 454, 1476
China, history of 316
Chinese brush painting 26, 53, 161, 365, 805, 964, 1009, 1595, 1614, 1780, 1854, 1913, 2269, 2426
Churches, cathedrals and abbeys 244, 911, 1260, 1287, 1311, 1351, 1418, 1453, 1573, 1658, 1938, 2274, 2491
Cinque Ports, the 1846
Clarinet, the 2248
Clowning 1637
Cold War, the 2495
Colour mixing 2483
Composers 225, 2157
Computing, CAD 1387
Computing, databases 574, 1205
Computing, desk top publishing 612, 1130, 1297, 1758
Computing, PowerPoint 1003
Computing, spreadsheets 1187, 2500
Computing, website 1386, 1509
Computing, word processing 41, 678, 1864, 2180, 2261
Computing 130, 146, 207, 209, 312, 322, 385, 483, 501, 910, 919, 966, 988, 1044, 1076, 1097, 1112, 1331, 1459, 1587, 1785, 1881, 2056, 2093, 2263, 2329, 2486
Conducting 565
Conwy, the river 1812
Cookery, bread and yeast 128
Cookery, Chinese 332
Cookery, French country 2549, 2690, 2769, 2774
Cookery, gourmet 88, 183, 186, 538, 1147, 2304, 2440
Cookery, hedgerow 2282
Cookery, Japanese 40
Cookery 936, 2442, 2536, 2568, 2609, 2655, 2727, 2736
Cotswolds, the 1919
Counselling 83, 976, 1293, 2247, 2480
Country house, the 366, 983, 1059, 1266, 1328, 1348, 1568, 1581, 1841, 2313, 2367
Countryside, the 31, 39, 178, 216, 367, 1184, 1323, 1391, 1497, 1511, 1770, 1788, 1883, 1942

Creation's stories with words and colour 1628
Crete 65, 2546
Cromwell, Oliver 2351, 2474
Croquet 596, 874, 982, 1159, 1440, 1447, 1491, 2121, 2218
Cuba 2684
Cumbria 2026
Cycling and walking 1734, 1955, 2299
Cycling 221, 1029, 2448
Cyprus 2547
Dales, the 1643, 1809
Dancing, ballroom 219, 359, 566, 1070, 2374
Dancing, belly 660, 944, 1764, 2527
Dancing, circle 1027, 2706, 2771
Dancing, folk 869, 1052, 1494, 2028, 2401, 2452
Dancing, Greek folk 2707, 2765
Dancing, line 200, 352, 571, 2178
Dancing, Scottish country 21, 371, 951, 2029, 2030, 2455, 2529
Dancing 87, 1307, 1774, 1895, 220, 373, 647, 676, 762, 2152, 2700, 2712
Danish whitework 905
Dante 2569, 2728, 2737
Dartmoor 724, 1457
de Compostela, Santiago 2571
Decorative interiors and paint effects 89, 540, 1475, 2371, 2443
Découpage 504
Demon drink, the 1367
Derbyshire 1341, 1355
Devon 546, 846, 1569, 1724, 1893
Diaghilev 56, 59
Discovery and adventure 1721, 2074, 2075
Discovery and creation 194
Diving 930, 1062, 1364, 1801, 1852
Doll's houses 806, 839
Dordogne, the 2629, 2647, 2671, 2685, 2749, 2766
Dowsing and divining 2092, 2420
Dragonflies and damselflies 994, 995, 1399
Drama 154, 170, 749, 1286, 1288, 1358, 1718
Drawing and painting, landscape 99, 1170, 1548, 1765, 1768, 1873, 2228, 2415
Drawing and painting, life 681

Drawing and painting, nature 884, 989, 1574, 1607, 2090
Drawing and painting, pastels 285
Drawing and painting 37, 164, 179, 228, 1327, 1555, 1670, 1823, 1925, 2054, 2235
Drawing and sketching 389, 774, 2412
Drawing and walking 931, 2124
Drawing and watercolour 1277, 1951, 2514
Drawing, buildings 876, 1080
Drawing, cartoons 106
Drawing, life 255, 432, 1378, 1747, 2199, 2470
Drawing, nature 2413
Drawing, portraits 2324
Drawing 58, 182, 268, 478, 502, 598, 637, 823, 924, 1146, 1171, 1188, 1438, 1507, 1641, 1685, 1917, 2172, 2389, 2435, 2517, 2535, 2566, 2607, 2654, 2726, 2735
Dry stone walling 344, 827, 1149, 1439, 1808, 2018
Durham 2275
Dvorak, Anton 2249
Dyeing 282, 850, 1886
Earth energy 112
East Anglia 1454, 1565, 1705, 1706, 1842, 2332
East Midlands 1580
Eastern promise 2015
Ecology and the environment 696, 745, 811, 1443, 1546, 1571, 1806, 1823, 1903, 2038, 2346, 2488, 2661
Edinburgh Festival 1827, 1921, 2021, 2022, 2112
Egypt 27, 898, 981, 1023, 1241, 1242, 2151, 2153, 2258
Elgar, Edward 557, 940, 1291, 1419, 1971, 2270, 2273, 2447
Embroidered boxes 1646
Embroidery, machine 193, 1192, 1686, 2175, 2365
Embroidery: C&G 414, 609, 1012, 1104
Embroidery 51, 117, 545, 679, 801, 826, 851, 1000, 1042, 1127, 1405, 1879, 1944, 2209, 2246
Enamelling 1550, 1640, 1689, 2396
England, history of 516, 620, 623, 813, 906, 1207, 1263, 1586

England 148, 969
English 939, 1518, 2127, 2323
Entertaining with ease 768
Esperanto 626, 1824, 1825, 1922, 1992
Euripides' Bacchae 2189
European Enlightenment 2146
European Renaissance 1965
Fabric covered boxes 592, 1472, 2132, 2479
Fabric craft 445, 604, 2224
Family activities 1807, 1900
Family adventure 1907
Family arts and crafts 1677
Family birdwatching 136, 241, 242, 246, 486
Family cycling and walking 1838
Family discovery 1631, 1918, 2156
Family drawing and painting 1796
Family holiday 2003
Family learning break 54, 752
Family music making 2032
Family nature discovery 300, 493, 1536, 1814, 1908, 2009
Family painting and drawing 2061
Family sketching 1738
Family wildlife discovery 1608, 1627, 1861, 1957, 2060, 2063, 2142
Faulks, Sebastian 515
Feltmaking 259, 784
Feng Shui 226, 600
Ferns 1398, 1645, 1950
Field survey 1866
Film festival 1920
Film making 674, 1974
Film studies 68, 157, 368, 1389, 1435, 1717, 1757, 2428, 2485
Finance 144, 310, 601, 1113, 1508, 1784
First aid 1411
Fishing 1534
Florence 2564, 2606, 2652, 2733
Flowers 576, 1247, 1324, 1532, 1610, 1906, 2013
Flute, the 1623, 2077, 2678
Folk 52, 2185, 2321
Follies and mad hatters 2391
Fossils 722, 1344
French 6, 361, 402, 537, 677, 757, 791, 807, 808, 1269, 1762, 2069, 2213, 2328, 2340, 2539, 2544, 2550, 2557, 2582, 2593, 2598, 2632, 2642, 2658, 2666, 2675, 2682, 2691, 2696, 2703, 2710, 2718, 2742, 2754, 2764, 2770, 2775
Fungi 735, 2406, 2424, 2475, 2509
Furniture care and restoration 570, 675, 886, 956, 1227, 1611, 1773, 2166, 2201
Furniture design 1428
Furniture making 946, 1949, 2281, 2305
Furniture 956
Garden design 343, 544, 639, 1490, 2285
Gardening 48, 175, 188, 354, 452, 513, 534, 577, 651, 865, 928, 935, 1034, 1045, 1046, 1073, 1150, 1216, 1332, 1575, 1578, 1618, 1676, 1745, 1976, 2217, 2291, 2364, 2444, 2520
Gardens 129, 700, 1178, 1218, 1708, 1805
Genealogy 398, 422, 495, 1424
Geology 315, 339, 1535, 1563, 1572, 2101, 2144, 2528
Georgians, the 1843, 2187
German 69, 323, 383, 1028, 1040, 1088, 1206, 2350, 2501
Germany 2638
Gibraltar 2758
Gilbert and Sullivan 1697, 1741, 2027
Gilding 1276
Glass, lakes and steam 1458
Glasscraft 430, 477, 926, 1015, 1133, 2138, 2513, 2515
Gold thread embroidery 396, 412, 1001
Golf 104, 273, 656, 1489, 1503, 1968
Gothic illuminated manuscripts 2476
Gothic in England, the 1421
Graphic illustration 401, 1413
Graphology 38, 295, 597, 1517, 2404
Grasses, sedges and rushes 301, 777, 878, 882, 1200, 1402, 1556
Great Exhibition and the Crystal Palace, the 685
Great expectations 1365
Greece 2575
Greek and Latin 1600
Greek 314, 405, 603, 2344, 2427, 2594, 2616, 2625, 2746, 2776
Greeks, the 1175
Green man, the 525, 1570, 2272
Guernsey 2553
Guitar, the 159, 1082, 1729, 2174
Hadrian's Wall 970, 1564
Haiku 1111
Hardy, Thomas 1309, 1707

Harp, the 142, 1622
Harpsichord, the 615, 1194
Health and fitness 86, 123, 308, 329, 376, 512, 555, 1002, 1005, 1138, 1204, 1298, 1605, 1782, 1844, 2120, 2338, 2449
Hebrides, the 650, 1290, 1592, 2303
Herachlus 1800
Herbs 2318
Heroes journey, the 2330
Hexham 469
Hieroglyphics 96
High peaks 2115
Higham informal gathering 243
History, local 291, 617
History, natural 584, 960, 1258, 1799
History, social 321, 897, 1120, 1128, 1189, 1305, 1450, 1579, 1713, 1740, 2131, 2352, 2397
History, transport 1007, 1121
History 1352
Hitchcock, Alfred 294
Holland 2600
Holy Land, the 1657, 2551
Homeopathy 890, 915
Horse riding 698, 1862, 2122
Iberian river: the Ebro 2576
Images of an island 2595
In search of the picturesque 838
In the shadow of the Dome 427
India 1004
Insects 425, 582, 775, 1644, 1977, 2202, 2369
Interior design 181, 185, 539, 790, 933, 1652
Internet, the 201, 272, 296, 543, 602, 893, 1089, 1109, 1711, 2265, 2339, 2355, 2405
Invertebrates 1860, 1981, 2084, 2155
Ireland 792, 2577, 2648, 2667, 2672
Irish 2554, 2611, 2628, 2637, 2646, 2659, 2668, 2676, 2683, 2687, 2697, 2704, 2711
Islands, birds and boating 634, 1528
Isle of Man, the 1047, 1716
Isle of Wight, the 84, 171
Istanbul 2779
Italian 384, 403, 693, 1144, 1310, 1654, 1855, 2341, 2530, 2531, 2532, 2561, 2562, 2563, 2602, 2603, 2604, 2649, 2650, 2651, 2692, 2721, 2722, 2723, 2730, 2731, 2732

Japan 8
Japanese 91
Jazz 499, 526, 986, 1319, 1415, 1702
Jesus 1882
Jewellery making 535, 727, 1140, 1226, 1834, 2089, 2511
Jewellery 325, 618, 2286
Journalism 2541
Jung, Carl Gustav 2190
Kakkolistic 2147
Kent 1710, 1934
Keyboard, electronic 217, 643
King Cotton, rise and fall of 1163
King Priam and the cunning little vixen 624
Knitting, machine 261, 514, 523, 1967
Know your angels 1961
Korean War, the 1116
Lacemaking 24, 80, 143, 160, 214, 215, 289, 307, 498, 759, 871, 903, 1011, 1072, 1095, 1099, 1124, 1167, 1172, 1223, 1301, 1393, 1647, 1648, 1649, 1725, 1726, 1727, 1728, 1778, 1878, 1943, 2049, 2145, 2276, 2419, 2432, 2468, 2503
Lake District, the 695, 1151, 1720, 2024, 2025, 2096, 2114
Lancashire 974, 1553
Land of the prince bishops, the 1703
Landscape as panorama 1432
Landscape for the new millennium 1590
Latin 62, 621, 2068
Lawrence, D.H. 66
Lincoln 520
Lincolnshire 141, 744, 998
Literature 149, 682, 786, 812, 821, 860, 873, 1164, 1251, 1261, 1335, 1492, 1585, 1616, 1619, 1712, 2007, 2023, 2035, 2110, 2184, 2193, 2477, 2522
Liverpool 2430
Living in comfort 1871
Living off the land 133
London 521, 739, 962
Lundy 718
Machine embroidery: C&G 507, 1108
Mackintosh and Wright 1313
Mackintosh, Charles Rennie 558, 1936, 2171
Magdalen, Mary 1390
Mah Jong 1302, 1985
Malta 517

Mammals 392, 583, 778, 881, 996, 1195, 1776, 1959, 1978, 2086, 2252, 2416, 2492
Manchester 1022, 1353, 2037
Mandolin, the 71, 72
Map and compass 10, 94, 196, 439, 463, 748, 2294, 2446
Mapping the imagination 1434
Marquetry 1635
Mass, weight and volume 1485
Massachusetts 2720
Massage, meditation and relaxation 35, 82, 126, 785, 1191, 1519, 1991, 2245, 2336, 2756
Medieval pilgrimage 1845
Metalcraft 450, 1385, 2381
Michaelangelo 2533, 2724
Microscopy 578, 2162, 2243
Middle East, the 311
Millennium celebration 2149
Millennium summer 2195
Miniature furniture 1214
Missenden 1731
Monarch and laureate 641
Monks, sheep and drains 25
Monmouth 278
Monteverdi, Claudio 593
Moore, Henry 275
Morecambe Bay 771
Morris, William 1604
Mosaic 77, 327, 416, 437, 636, 889, 916, 1538, 1589, 1683, 1994, 2510, 2519
Mosses, lichens and liverworts 44, 589, 667, 782, 941, 1525, 1609, 1673, 1678, 1926, 2497
Mountains and waterfalls 2223
Mozart, Amadeus 165, 1083, 1787, 2670
Music and literature 885
Music and walking 716, 721, 725, 847, 1701, 1929
Music appreciation 36, 423, 429, 494, 605, 619, 794, 1141, 1292, 1602, 2080
Music 30, 121, 172, 211, 222, 238, 292, 408, 511, 564, 658, 673, 977, 1026, 1075, 1345, 1404, 1544, 1584, 1655, 1661, 1691, 1719, 1923, 1966, 1973, 2182, 2210, 2311, 2393, 2418, 2451, 2453, 2465, 2478
Musical instrument making 230

Myceneans, the 2590
National Trust, the 1939
National Vegetation Classification 298, 1481, 1523, 1905
Needlecraft 1273, 1914, 2466
Nelson, Horatio 407
New York 2540
Norfolk 1322
Normandy 2619
Normans, the 265, 1014
Northumbria 701, 1252, 1451, 1840
Norwich 822, 1566
Numerology 1783
Oboe, the 1877
Offa's Dyke 2010
Opera 64, 270, 668, 1071, 1074, 1122, 2119, 2244, 2471, 2570, 2693, 2729, 2738
Oral presentation skills 1444
Organ, the 1964
Orienteering 971
Origins of human civilisation 1577
Orkney 868
Otter, the 135, 1499
Owls 1990
Pacifism 761
Painting and drawing, farms 1284
Painting and drawing, landscape 705, 1909
Painting and drawing, nature 659, 1201
Painting and drawing, seascapes 1688
Painting and drawing 1816, 1924
Painting and literature 1915
Painting and prayer retreat 1068
Painting and relaxation 1982
Painting and sketching, boats and harbours 1233
Painting and sketching, nature 1143
Painting and sketching 328, 837, 1669, 2073, 2204, 2368
Painting miniatures and silhouettes 76, 434, 625, 927
Painting, boats and harbours 736, 1055, 1839, 2109, 2143, 2524
Painting, castles 856, 1599
Painting, coastal landscapes 1043, 1193
Painting, gouache 1797
Painting, landscape and drawing 2008
Painting, landscape and nature 97
Painting, landscape and still life 205

Painting, landscape 204, 253, 444, 449, 459, 548, 549, 569, 644, 648, 649, 706, 712, 720, 852, 866, 949, 968, 1050, 1061, 1153, 1154, 1155, 1161, 1253, 1256, 1257, 1280, 1306, 1326, 1340, 1446, 1448, 1482, 1559, 1560, 1561, 1594, 1674, 1698, 1699, 1700, 1743, 1804, 1822, 1870, 1927, 1930, 1941, 1956, 2005, 2031, 2105, 2160, 2207, 2221, 2289, 2297, 2300, 2302, 2306, 2382, 2460, 2580

Painting, life 421, 1612

Painting, miniature 857, 2150, 2484

Painting, nature 109, 206, 213, 256, 276, 374, 379, 400, 465, 586, 591, 799, 1158, 1198, 1303, 1417, 1430, 1766, 1898, 1997, 2059, 2211, 2219, 2333, 2337, 2366, 2386, 2512, 2523

Painting, oils and acrylics 120, 326, 489, 1212, 1739, 1786, 1889, 2226, 2241

Painting, pastels 125, 218, 348, 418, 552, 1557, 1662, 1858, 2085, 2257, 2379, 2388, 2392, 2507

Painting, portrait 800, 917, 921, 963, 1065, 1272, 1321, 1478, 1887, 2398

Painting, seascapes 346, 646

Painting, still life 224, 336, 819

Painting 4, 13, 15, 93, 95, 107, 167, 197, 234, 355, 447, 510, 614, 702, 728, 737, 746, 747, 849, 953, 975, 1114, 1132, 1174, 1237, 1283, 1346, 1371, 1377, 1474, 1483, 1516, 1748, 1749, 1802, 1853, 1859, 1865, 1885, 1912, 1999, 2004, 2033, 2062, 2064, 2141, 2345, 2348, 2395, 2537, 2542, 2548, 2556, 2560, 2572, 2578, 2581, 2591, 2599, 2614, 2623, 2630, 2640, 2656, 2664, 2673, 2680, 2689, 2694, 2701, 2708, 2716, 2740, 2752, 2762, 2768, 2773

Palaeography 1118

Papercraft 67, 137, 139, 482, 653, 835, 1471, 1760, 1986, 2082, 2181, 2438

Papier maché 932

Parchment craft 640

Passementerie 45, 102, 531, 1275, 2287

Past life regression 2045

Patchwork and quilting: C&G 505, 608, 1103

Patchwork 1407, 1477, 1562

Peak District, the 189

Pembrokeshire 750, 1527, 1693, 1694, 1894, 2161

Personal development 22, 57, 176, 751, 795, 967, 1294, 1412, 1414, 1952, 2260, 2456, 2645, 2745

Peru 2552

Philosophy 815, 1008, 2357

Photography, black and white 804, 2315

Photography, colour 269, 2436

Photography, digital 210, 769, 877, 1217, 1824

Photography, landscape 131, 177, 732, 1902, 2231

Photography, nature 236, 369, 635, 666, 772, 832, 861, 993, 1152, 1531, 1671, 1679, 2370, 2437

Photography, portrait 485

Photography 1051, 1137, 1179, 1231, 1329, 1400, 1449, 1514, 245, 297, 331, 358, 462, 661, 950, 1540, 1672, 1695, 1756, 1821, 1928, 2376, 2459, 2516, 2636, 2747

Piano, the 338, 496, 760, 978, 1373, 1777, 1869, 2334

Picos de Europa 2610

Picture framing and mounting 550, 985, 2325, 2390, 2457

Plants 1037, 1196, 1520, 1664, 2000

Plasterwork 1495, 1660, 2423

Plato 1117

Poetry 70, 127, 662, 1427, 1467, 1704, 2113

Poland 2589, 2744

Pondweeds 997

Portfolio preparation 1375

Pottery and porcelain restoration: C&G 413, 1105

Pottery and print making 1, 353, 754, 1243, 1744, 2170

Pottery 3, 73, 90, 257, 431, 436, 542, 843, 954, 955, 1181, 1229, 1244, 1362, 1593, 1820, 1832, 1940, 2048, 2216, 2360, 2372, 2377, 2384, 2518

Prague 2588

Preparing working designs: C&G 1010

Pre-Raphaelites, the 23, 1356

Printmaking 864, 1110, 1751, 2309, 2429

Psychology 399, 1488, 1656, 2094

Pyrenees, the 2713, 2739

Quilting 20, 1835, 2417
Rachmaninov, Sergei 318
Raffiawork 428, 1308
Railways 948, 1156, 1316, 1343, 1433, 2079, 2118, 2206, 2298
Rambling 108, 260, 2002
Recorder, the 18, 60, 284, 378, 460, 1077, 1347, 1408, 1420, 2284
Reiki 306, 476, 892, 1638, 2057
Relaxology 2585
Religion 232, 424, 669, 914, 1176, 1190, 1279, 2036, 2196, 2271
Remarque, Erich Maria 863
Rhetoric 913
Ribble Way, the 714
Riding 2164, 2165
Rock climbing 575, 1090, 1397, 2408
Romania 2597, 2639
Romans, the 1456, 1598
Rome 1962, 2748
Royal Navy, history of the 2335
Russia 2715
Russian 5, 63, 147, 360, 404, 756, 1268, 1761, 2212, 2342
Sabah 2760
Sacred clowning 1500
Sacred Gaia 1636
Saxophone, the 1078, 2053
Scagliola 1285
Schubert, Franz 999
Schumann, Robert 2194
Scotland, history of 288, 1165, 1337, 1357, 1715, 1826, 1935, 1937, 2039, 2040
Scotland 1186, 1336, 1441, 1545, 1576, 1681
Scottish Gaelic 1267, 1361
Scottish waterways 723, 2148
Scrabble® and walking 1368
Scrabble® 945, 2220
Screen printing and dye painting 1220
Scriptwriting 2643
Sculpture 16, 456, 934, 1066, 1383, 1384, 1539, 1755, 2099, 2439, 2461, 2574
Seashore, the 81, 1019, 1058, 1888, 1970, 2128, 2192
Severn Way, the 1904
Shakespeare, William 622, 740, 1168, 2091
Sherlock Holmes and the Victorian detective 118, 313, 2354
Shropshire 711, 972

Silk painting 11, 33, 124, 333, 395, 530, 684, 707, 1182, 1185, 1202, 1794, 2359, 2402, 2458
Silk screen printing 1684
Silver odyssey, a 1714
Silversmithing and goldsmithing 471
Silversmithing and jewellery 98, 1274, 2136, 2347
Silversmithing 2, 79, 435, 630, 652, 842, 925, 1064, 1245, 1818, 2016, 2197, 2215, 2363, 2493
Silverwork 202
Singing 28, 150, 163, 223, 290, 394, 474, 500, 590, 594, 642, 665, 715, 787, 840, 918, 979, 1162, 1183, 1221, 1318, 1395, 1629, 1668, 1972, 1995, 2240, 2319, 2349, 2400
Sisters of the British 689
Sketching and painting 841
Sketching and walking 683, 1039
Sketching, portrait 738
Sketching 115, 568, 1429
Snowdonia 734, 1811, 1825, 2001, 2012
Somerset 1632, 1872, 2078
Sound recording 320, 581, 2312
South Africa 2767
Spain 518, 1304
Spanish 406, 417, 426, 573, 1016, 1282, 1911, 2343
Spiders 2232, 2251, 2445
Spinal touch 980
Spinning and weaving 274, 281, 1086, 1436, 1916, 2714
St Petersburg 2103, 2200
Stained glass 184, 187, 212, 330, 551, 599, 638, 923, 937, 1020, 1041, 1123, 1134, 1148, 1208, 1333, 1460, 1480, 1542, 1769, 2017, 2264, 2290, 2361, 2373, 2378
Steam in the south west 2100
Stick making 162, 870
Stone carving 340, 1180, 1246, 1382, 1687, 2133, 2441, 2633
Stone circles 132
Stonecraft 2362
Stress and spirituality 961
Stringed instruments 377, 473, 872, 1295, 1445, 1487, 1771, 2098, 2322
Stumpwork embroidery:C&G 506, 1106

Stumpwork 2255
Suffolk 119, 388, 1521, 1663, 2414
Summer activity 1530, 1896
Summer read 1591
Sussex 370, 645, 1238, 1369, 1680, 2506
Svalbard 2559
Swimming 480, 765, 1254, 2163, 2326
T'ai Chi Chuan 1024, 1789
T'ai Chi 397, 438, 443, 464, 560, 1248, 2422, 2499
T'ai Ji Quan & Chinese health arts 606
Tailoring 559, 789, 1596, 1880, 1945, 2496
Tale telling 2327
Tapestry 1380, 1752, 1828
Tarot 1469
Tatting 492
Teddy bear making 816, 904, 2087
Tennyson, Alfred 337
Textile decorative techniques: C&G 610, 1013
Textiles 1396, 1549, 1625, 1753
Theatre 335, 1543, 1624, 1793, 2239, 2292, 2317, 2469
Thomas, Edward 1018
Tiffany lampshade making 703, 1289
Tile making and renovation 1874
Town and country planning in Britain 451
Trees and woodland 252, 710, 770, 833, 883, 912, 1465, 1630, 1980, 2225, 2288
Trojans, the 2183
Trollope miniaturist 1126
Tuscany 2719
Tutankhamun 277
Um-Cha-Cha 2046
Upholstery 802, 1035, 1063, 1370
Utopias: 11th annual Raymond Williams 527
Verdi, Giuseppe 293
Victorians, the 1025, 1850
Vienna 1006
Vikings, the 688, 1372
Villas and gardens 2734
Viol consort 375, 1374
Visual impairment 446, 2421
Vivaldi, Antonio 1837
Wagner, Richard 896
Wales 1056, 1057, 1848
Walking and bridge 458
Walking and natural history 1496
Walking and sketching 2034

Walking in the Charente 2538, 2543, 2558, 2573, 2579, 2583, 2592, 2615, 2624, 2631, 2641, 2657, 2665, 2674, 2681, 2695, 2702, 2709, 2717, 2741, 2753, 2763
Walking with barn dancing 1339
Walking with Ceilidh dancing 442, 2375, 2525
Walking 267, 419, 487, 580, 663, 708, 875, 894, 992, 1094, 1169, 1236, 1259, 1320, 1815, 1910, 1932, 1979, 2014, 2081, 2117, 2295, 2316, 2380, 2411, 2555, 2587, 2612, 2618, 2669, 2677, 2698, 2705, 2750, 2757, 2778
Walton, William 1354
Wansfell 1515
War by sea and on land 1792
Watercolour and gouache, landscape 798
Watercolour and gouache, nature 457
Watercolour and pastels 563
Watercolour, harbourside 836
Watercolour, landscape and seascape 2227
Watercolour, landscape 529, 664, 854, 891, 1969, 2567, 2608
Watercolour, nature 240, 264, 363, 1234, 1317, 1733
Watercolour, still life 1547
Watercolour: C&G 410, 900, 1211
Watercolour 19, 43, 74, 78, 101, 152, 251, 258, 263, 283, 350, 387, 488, 553, 554, 579, 585, 631, 655, 741, 828, 859, 880, 907, 908, 938, 958, 984, 1030, 1036, 1067, 1081, 1092, 1173, 1199, 1232, 1366, 1401, 1426, 1470, 1510, 1524, 1730, 1736, 1750, 1791, 1803, 1819, 1833, 1857, 1890, 1946, 1987, 1996, 2006, 2052, 2083, 2116, 2140, 2203, 2230, 2242, 2250, 2266, 2277, 2279, 2307, 2310, 2394, 2425, 2433, 2462, 2489
Waterways 1682
Welsh 7, 362, 758, 1270, 1763, 2214
Wessex 1349, 1423
West Country, the 468, 1350, 2236
Westonbirt 1554, 1692
Whisky trail 2450
Whist and walking 2111, 2158
Wild flowers 195, 386, 391, 467, 697, 733, 773, 809, 830, 879, 929, 965, 1264, 1334, 1675, 1813, 1892

Wild man of the woods, the 1849
Wilde, Oscar 1084, 1224
Wildlife 334, 470, 587, 776, 780, 959, 973, 991, 1160, 1197, 1235, 1281, 1431, 1526, 1626, 1737, 1767, 1875, 2067, 2205, 2283, 2487, 2622, 2761
Williams, Vaughan 2095
Willowcraft 14, 532, 829, 1506
Wind instruments 192, 671, 763, 1096, 1278, 2055, 2237
Windmills 1299
Wine appreciation 509, 633, 1406, 1659, 2267
Wonderful water 503
Woodcarving: C&G 415, 803, 1215
Woodcarving 632, 743, 1038, 1541, 1613, 1667, 1732
Woodcraft 249, 433, 536, 541, 629, 730, 1230, 1468, 2047, 2051, 2167, 2168, 2383, 2434
Woodwind and brass playing 717, 726
Woolf, Virginia 46
Working and playing with nature spirits 783
Working towards sustainability 2233
World War I 50, 2130

World War II 888, 1452
Writing, autobiography 364, 680, 686
Writing, comedy for television 1102
Writing, creative 305, 952, 1017, 1250, 1360, 1567, 1817, 1998, 2070, 2399
Writing, feature 1296
Writing, fiction 1484
Writing, fiction 2504
Writing, film 796
Writing, magazine articles 607
Writing, novel 381, 1271, 1954, 2627
Writing, poetry 409, 627
Writing, radio 895
Writing, science fiction and fantasy 1210, 1513
Writing, travel 158, 2584, 2743
Writing 235, 299, 319, 561, 767, 1325, 1410, 1463, 1582, 1933, 1963, 2066, 2256, 2472, 2634, 2755
Yellow composites 1498
Yoga and walking 2123
Yoga 110, 303, 349, 372, 479, 1049, 1416, 1493, 2596
York 2042
Yorkshire 753, 1119, 1249, 1901, 2191